PRAISE FOR BUILDING EFFECTIVE VALUE CHAINS

'Tom and I have discussed over many years how best to develop shared business process and data standards whereby customers and suppliers, including competitors, can best design and run modern supply chains to serve the consumer more cost-effectively. More recently we have debated what we should mean by value and how best it can be realized through sound management. I trust this book will stimulate you to look afresh at your value chains.'
Sir Iain Anderson, former Director of Unilever for Strategy and Technology

'Tom and I worked together to introduce modern supply chain management into Rowntree Mackintosh and Nestlé. The practical results were substantial in terms of customer service, inventory management and supplier relationships. We place particular emphasis on sound data defined in such a way as to promote effective joint management of our value chain. I commend this book for your value chains.'
Peter Blackburn CBE, former Chairman of Rowntree Mackintosh and Chief Executive of Nestlé France, then Nestlé UK. Sometime president of the Food and Drink Federation

'Professor McGuffog, a leading authority on value chain management, provides a state-of-the-art analysis of the subject. He looks at the problems it has experienced in the past, using specific examples, and how it can be utilized to improve performance in the future in the private, public, and charitable sectors of the economy and society. It is a must-read for all managers.'
Professor Lord Smith of Clifton

'Tom chaired the group at GS1 (formerly Article Number Association and e.centre) which developed the key standards and network for Electronic Data Interchange which have served business well for three decades. He has worked actively as a Fellow of the Chartered Institute of Logistics and Transport including chairing its Value Chain Forum. This book will be essential reading for all those concerned with Value and its management.'
Jim Spittle, President of CILT, Chairman of GS1UK, former Group Supply Chain Director of Kingfisher, and Director of Tesco

Building Effective Value Chains

Building Effective Value Chains
Value and its management

Tom McGuffog

LONDON PHILADELPHIA NEW DELHI

Publisher's note

Every possible effort has been made to ensure that the information contained in this book is accurate at the time of going to press, and the publishers and authors cannot accept responsibility for any errors or omissions, however caused. No responsibility for loss or damage occasioned to any person acting, or refraining from action, as a result of the material in this publication can be accepted by the editor, the publisher or the author.

First published in Great Britain and the United States in 2016 by Kogan Page Limited

Apart from any fair dealing for the purposes of research or private study, or criticism or review, as permitted under the Copyright, Designs and Patents Act 1988, this publication may only be reproduced, stored or transmitted, in any form or by any means, with the prior permission in writing of the publishers, or in the case of reprographic reproduction in accordance with the terms and licences issued by the CLA. Enquiries concerning reproduction outside these terms should be sent to the publishers at the undermentioned addresses:

2nd Floor, 45 Gee Street	1518 Walnut Street, Suite 1100	4737/23 Ansari Road
London	Philadelphia PA 19102	Daryaganj
EC1V 3RS	USA	New Delhi 110002
United Kingdom		India

© Tom McGuffog 2016

The right of Tom McGuffog to be identified as the author of this work has been asserted by him in accordance with the Copyright, Designs and Patents Act 1988.

ISBN   978 0 7494 7376 1
E-ISBN 978 0 7494 7377 8

British Library Cataloguing-in-Publication Data

A CIP record for this book is available from the British Library.

Library of Congress Control Number

2016943588

Typeset by Graphicraft Limited, Hong Kong
Print production managed by Jellyfish
Printed and bound in Great Britain by CPI Group (UK) Ltd, Croydon CR0 4YY

CONTENTS

About the author xi
Acknowledgements xiii

01 Realizing value and value chain management 1

Executive summary 1
Your value chain can become far more valuable 2
Value 7

02 Introduction 8

03 Overarching values 13

Summary 13
Giving life to values 13
Relative values 14
A valuable conclusion 16

04 The optimal sequence of decisions 18

Summary 19
The decision sequence 19

05 The value in value chain management 22

Summary 22
Definition 22
How to do more with less – frugal innovation 25
Value chain linkages and interactions 25
Value chain management measures 25
Valuing human life 26
Stocks and flows 27
Net present value 27
Earned value management 28

Transfer prices 29
Conclusions on value 29

06 A review of some modern value chains 31

6A Finance, food, automotive, electronics 31

6A.1 The financial value chain 31
6A.2 The food value chain 41
6A.3 The automotive value chain 49
6A.4 The electronics value chain 55

6B Public sector, health, defence equipment, public transport, water 60

6B.1 The public sector value chain 60
6B.2 Health and care value chains 65
6B.3 Defence equipment (materiel) value chain 77
6B.4 Passenger transport – rail, road, air, sea 84
6B.5 The water value chain: structure and added value 89

6C Reform of key institutions 99

6C.1 Reform of the government value chain 99
6C.2 Reforming our democratic value chain 111

6D Voluntary and charitable, sport, the arts 116

6D.1 Voluntary and charitable sector value chains 116
6D.2 Sports club value chain 127
6D.3 The arts value chains 130

07 A question of identity 135

Introduction 135
Barcodes 136
Master data 137
Electronic business 138
Banking 141

Electronic tags and RFID 142
Healthcare identification 142
Building and maintaining aircraft 143
Defence 145
A better future for us all 145
Identify us well 146

08 Constructing sound value chain process and data architectures 149

Introduction 149
Structuring the process architecture 150
The plan to payment process 151
Defining a sound data architecture 156
Single window 161
Financial flows 161
Recommendations 162
Value chain process analysis and driving business change 163

09 Value chain collaboration and competition 165

Introduction to competition and collaboration issues – legal and practical 165
9A Staying within the law 165
9B Effective value chain collaboration and competition 170

10 Effective and integrated value chain planning 176

Summary 176
Dynamic planning 177
Integrated business planning 179

11 Managing uncertainty 182

Introduction 182
Definitions 185
Uncertainty explored 188

Uncertainty and lack of understanding   191
Attitudes to uncertainty, opportunity and risk   191
Integrated planning and risk methodology   193
Risk lists and matrices   196

12 Dynamic management of projects and initiatives   198

Methodology   199
Application to financial investment and to value chain operations management   207
Conclusion   208

13 Valuable steps to success and future value chain R&D   209

Twelve practical steps to success   209
Proposed areas for value chain research and development   211

14 Practical exercises in value chain management   215

Exercise 1   215
Exercise 2   216
Exercise 3   216
Exercise 4   216
Exercise 5   217

15 Key references   218

15A Value chain management references   218

Index   225

ABOUT THE AUTHOR

Following a very sound schooling at Hermitage Academy in Helensburgh, Tom studied Political Economy and Political Science at the University of Glasgow and then completed a postgraduate degree at the University of Massachusetts in Amherst. Thereafter he worked as an economist in the electricity industry in London and Liverpool on econometric forecasting, pricing and planning. In 1967 he joined Rowntree in York to undertake operational research, redesign of sales operations and of terms of trading, and systems development.

Tom has been involved in the development of modern value chain management since the early days. In the 1970s he began work with colleagues across the UK at the Article Number Association (latterly e.centre and then GS1UK, of which he is an honorary life member) on the design of systems for identifying traded items, supply chain locations and individuals. He chaired the group which developed the key standards and messages for Electronic Data Interchange and which developed the main UK EDI network.

In the 1980s he led the introduction of modern supply chain management into Rowntree Mackintosh as Director of Transport and Distribution, Planning, Logistics, Purchasing and IT. Similar roles followed in the 1990s with Nestlé where he was Director of IT, Planning, Logistics, and Electronic Business.

In parallel he was Vice Chairman of the Simpler Trade Procedures Board at the Department for Trade and Industry, and Head of Delegation to the United Nations in Geneva for Trade Facilitation and Electronic Business. He chaired UK Partners for Electronic Business which included the key standards bodies – e.centre, APACS (banking), Cabinet Office, SITPRO, DTI, British Standards Institution, and also the UK Council for Electronic Business (which is responsible for standards relating to engineering, aerospace and defence developments – Tom is an honorary life member). He was awarded the MBE in 2002 for his contributions to the development of global electronic business.

He has also had wide involvement in the public sector. He was invited to be a member of the Ministerial Advisory Council of the NHS Purchasing and Supply Agency (PASA) and latterly the Audit Committee. He served as a board member of Selby & York Primary Care Trust, and continues to support UK health as an Associate Mental Health Manager sitting on Appeal Panels. He has also served on Inland Revenue Appeal Panels.

Tom was invited in 1999 to be the first non-executive director of the Defence Procurement Agency and served for seven years, including chairing the Audit Committee. With colleagues he advanced the definition and management of projects and of risk. He also served on the board of the Defence Logistics Organisation.

Tom was Visiting Professor for Management and Electronic Business at the University of Glasgow and Visiting Senior Fellow at the University of Bath. He is pleased to have been asked to deliver an annual lecture on supply chain management at the Royal Holloway College of the University of London to the students of cryptography (according to Dan Brown in the *The Da Vinci Code* the French detective Sophie Neveu studied cryptography at Royal Holloway). Tom continues to work with the Chartered Institute of Logistics and Transport of which he is a Fellow. Farther along the value chain he is also a Fellow of the Chartered Institute of Procurement and Supply.

Tom works actively with several charitable, voluntary, sports, musical and bibliographic bodies. His first of many signed copies of books was given to him by Igor Sikorsky when he did a stint in production control at Sikorsky Helicopters.

The name McGuffog is an ancient Galloway name. Sir Patrick McGuffog aided Robert the Bruce to become King of Scotland. One of their lands is Guffogland near Castle Douglas. Hugh McGuffog of Castle Rusco was High Sheriff of Galloway from 1689 to 1700. Tom's father John McGuffog received his British Empire Medal (BEM) for his work in shipbuilding from King George VI at Buckingham Palace in 1943.

ACKNOWLEDGEMENTS

The particular genesis of this book is the publication prepared with my colleagues in the Value Chain Forum of the Chartered Institute of Logistics and Transport (CILT) – 'Value Chain Management – Developing a More Valuable and Certain Future' by Tom McGuffog, Barry Evans, Peter Jordan, Jeremy Clarke, Nick Wadsley et al. including Sha Alavi, Bill Brockbank, Andy Chapell, Richard Ellithorne, Malcolm Iles, Ed Kuzemko, David Meggitt, Gordon Milne, Callum Moy, Barry Orum, Ben Waller and Phil Wood.

I am especially grateful to Barry Evans of the Cardiff Business School, ex-Tesco, for continuing to provide a major stimulus to my work.

CILT and its President James Spittle, its Chief Executive Steve Agg, and Ana Walker have been most encouraging. Also supportive have been GS1 (President Lord Philip Hunt, Chairman Jim Spittle (again), Chief Executive Gary Lynch and directors Andrew Osborne, Alaster Purchase and Holly Porter).

Paralleling GS1's work on identities and e-business for products and people is UKCeB's work in the fields of engineering and aerospace. I am very grateful to colleagues there and notably to the Chief Executive Steve Shepherd.

The Chartered Institute of Procurement and Supply (Chief Executive David Noble) continues to stimulate me, as does the Institute of Directors (Director General Simon Walker and Chief Economist James Sproule).

Outstanding support has come from my wife (Sheila – mother, nurse and midwife, and associate hospital chaplain), and from my family value chain – Iain (Chief Economist South West Water and now Director of Ofwat) and his wife Rebecca (hospital administrator); Catriona (marketing and sales consultant to technology companies) and her husband Don (senior scientist at DEFRA advising government agricultural research establishments across several continents); Douglas (excellent photomedia designer, including for many of my publications) and his partner Samantha (style designer); and Alison (psychologist specializing in people within defence and security) and her husband Antony (also expert in psychology in relation to security involving government and transport across the world). I am receiving increasing advice from our grandchildren Anna, Ben, Louis and Albert.

My background in economics came from the Universities of Glasgow (Principal Anton Muscatelli and Professor Sir Laurie Hunter) and Massachusetts (my professor friend Marshall Howard is still golfing at 94). A fellow graduate of both institutions is my friend Sir Iain Anderson with whom I continue to debate value and its management.

I learned much at The Electricity Council and the Merseyside and North Wales Electricity Board. My work on Supply Chain Management and Electronic Business began at Rowntree Mackintosh in the 1970s and gathered pace in the 1980s, and thereafter at Nestlé in the 1990s. Among the many inspiring colleagues were Sir Donald Barron, Peter Blackburn, Arzilia Da Silva, Peter Denton, Ken Dixon, Ian Hill, Stan Hogg, Robin Kidd, Peter Lawson, John Pearson, Nigel Pells, Stuart Roberts, Jack Sinclair, Ken Stephens, John Sunley and Chris Tyas. It would be invidious to mention my many sparring partners (sorry, value chain partners) in our customers and suppliers, and in competitors, without whom effective value chains cannot develop.

I was very fortunate in my non-executive roles to work on trade facilitation and electronic business with Ray Walker, Lord Jan Chelmsford and Sir Angus Fraser. On physical and mental health matters I worked with Prof Stuart Humby, Chris Reid, and Mike Wash among others. On defence I learned much from Lt Gen Andrew Figgures, David Gould, Sir Peter Spencer and Sir Robert Walmsley

My work with the voluntary sector (Section 6D.1) has been inspired by mission partners at St Columba's Community Foundation which I chair in York – BESOM (providing free furnishings for people getting their first accommodation); Family Matters (counselling couples with problems); The Island (mentoring children with difficulties at home and school); Reflect (pregnancy matters); Street Angels (rescuing those about to fall on Friday and Saturday nights); and York Neighbours who provide contact and support for the elderly. My friends Robin Garland (Project Mala) and John Jenkins (SportsAble) set great standards for invaluable help to those in great need.

I acknowledge gratefully my colleagues on the Committee of York Squash Rackets Club, and also those at Fulford (York) and Portpatrick (Galloway) Golf Clubs.

On matters of potential reform of government and key institutions I am most grateful to friends at the Reform Club in London and elsewhere, including Simon Blundell, Clem Brohier, Lord Nigel Jones, Arnold Rosen, Professor Lord Trevor Smith, Professor John Tate, Philip Taylor and Peter Urbach.

Realizing value and value change management

01

Executive summary

'Value' is one of the most important words we use. We value our home, our property, our business, our investments and our pension. More importantly, we value the lives of ourselves and of our families and friends. The former are much more straightforward to quantify than the latter. But without quantification (evaluation), how can we decide whether to buy or sell, set up or close a business, privatize or nationalize, pursue expensive medical treatments or preserve endangered habitats or creatures? If we find personal quantifications difficult, how much more difficult is it for us to judge decisions by governments or organizations which affect us significantly? Far too often, key decisions are made without explicit and agreed values and evaluations – to alter systems and facilities for health and social care, pensions and allowances, employment and pay, education, housing, justice and law and order, energy and other utilities such as water, transport, defence, population and immigration, foreign affairs and aid, research and development, support for the voluntary sector, sport, arts and culture, environment, communications and media. In business, how should we value the interests of employees, shareholders, directors, consumers, customers and suppliers, communities and nations?

Once again, we are at a critical stage for deciding what and how we value. Governments imply that all citizens are valued equally, but are often not prepared to define what this means in practical and financial terms nor to pay the corresponding bills, in relation to health and care, benefits, education, justice and other key expenditures. What value do we really place on citizens versus foreign residents (with and without funds), immigrants, people fleeing persecution, people drowning in people-smugglers' boats or dying at their homes from guns or famine? Furthermore, if we do care, what are the most effective value chains to put in place to achieve agreed objectives? What must the government manage, what should we leave to the markets, what should individuals be responsible for individually or collectively, and how do we define and manage everything else?

This book aims to assist business, government and individuals to define and calculate value more effectively and to manage its realization more efficiently. It also aims to support the voluntary and charitable sectors. This book intends to add value to students, teachers and researchers. Whatever you value, and whatever value chain you marshal and manage in order to realize your objectives, this is the book for you.

Your value chain can become far more valuable

Chapter 2 provides the introduction to value and its management – value in use and value in exchange. A value chain is the overall set of internal and external resources – human, physical, financial and informational – that require to be marshalled and managed in order to achieve the objectives of any organization.

Chapter 3 describes the overarching values which you may decide to use in your life, in your organization and across your value chain. What values really matter to you, your organization, your customers and suppliers, your employees, your shareholders and your stakeholders? How are you going to apply these values?

Chapter 4 defines the optimal sequence of decisions you should employ. Begin with agreed objectives (outcomes) and support their achievement by developing a rigorous set of internal and external business processes across your value chain. Support these by a well-defined data architecture – who is going to need what information, where and when. Only then consider reorganizations. Only thereafter develop new information and IT systems. In 21st-century value chain management, never begin with a reorganization.

Chapter 5 provides all the key definitions and measures across value chains.

Chapter 6 provides analyses of some key private, public and voluntary value chains. What are their core purposes, strategies, objectives, and measures of performance? We review the key factors and issues for each value chain. These examples should encourage you to undertake an analysis of your value chain. Help me and my colleagues to make valuable improvements. This chapter also encourages the reform of our key government and parliamentary value chains, and of other vital national institutions, in order to enhance the value of our democracy. Your thoughtful consideration of governmental processes should not occur only at election time.

Chapter 7 illustrates the vital importance of being able to identify all the goods and services, individuals and locations, across your value chain. I describe why and how these key components of value chain management came to be developed over the past half century. It's a question of identity.

Chapter 8 then defines in more detail how to construct effective process and data architectures.

Chapter 9 guides you on observing national and international competition laws. It also encourages best practice in collaborating with your value chain partners. You will always need to balance competition and collaboration within the law. What should you leave to market forces and what do you need to manage with your value chain partners?

Chapter 10 defines how to plan across your value chain in a structured manner. Remember, failing to plan is planning to fail.

Chapter 11 defines in a fresh and rigorous way the meaning of uncertainty, and of its key components opportunity and risk. Much risk management in the public and private sectors is poor, and there is always a danger that it becomes box ticking. The Treasury has yet to understand that an essential component of sound management is identifying, owning and managing your risks as well as your opportunities.

Chapter 12 develops an improved way to define and manage complex projects, initiatives and value chain operations. This describes how to define your requirements for performance (outcomes), total costs and timeliness, and how to trade off within and between each of these in order to achieve cost-effective success.

Chapter 13 summarizes the actions to take in order to build and operate a successful organization and value chain. This chapter also recommends further R&D.

Chapter 14 provides a set of exercises and projects for students and others to undertake in order to apply the ideas and techniques described in this book.

Chapter 15 provides a large set of references for further study. This should be of particular help to students and seekers after knowledge. Note that some particular references are provided at the end of certain chapters.

The most emotional value relates to human life. If an expensive drug or treatment improves lifespans by, say, one year on average, who should receive it – babies, children, young adults, workers, housewives, carers, the elderly, those who have paid their taxes, those on benefits, immigrants? If we increase the costs of energy here and now in order to reduce consumption and carbon emissions, what are the values to be placed on human lives saved and standards of living across the world in 50 years? If we attack another country, are their inhabitants' lives worth less than ours?

Less emotionally, but vitally important, are the values being pursued by all organizations and individuals. For too long we have not defined and measured value sufficiently well. This is a fresh attempt to do so.

Now is a particularly important time to re-address value and how we should optimize it. Many experts are finding it difficult to see from where fresh economic growth across the world is going to arise. What developments are going to add genuine value in a sustained way? After all, the well-off people in well-off countries have nearly all the things they need or even desire, while the poor everywhere do not have the wherewithal to pay for adequate healthcare, especially in childhood and old age, or for nutritional food, housing, education, justice, security, fuel, transport, and other goods and services which we take for granted. Growth has declined in the developing countries and is often stagnating in the advanced economies. Many of the current technological developments relate to fashion more than substance, such as those for personal devices and social media.

Therefore we should think afresh about the investments that will add genuine value across the globe. We need a new 'added-value arithmetic' in order to assess rigorously governmental and private sector (notably in finance) initiatives and projects. We require better ways to structure and analyse data instead of hoping that new technology will do this for us. Also, we need greatly improved value chain management to deliver benefits cost-effectively. This book addresses these issues and proposes solutions.

Value does not exist in isolation. It has to be considered alongside the following:

1 Core purpose, which is then broken down into specific objectives – what we are trying to achieve. What benefits are to be delivered, to whom and when?

2 What are our overarching values? Have we an agreed ethical or moral framework within which decisions will taken?

3 How are measures of value to be determined – by markets (local, national and international), official bodies, regulators, officials, government ministers, referendums? If, for example, share prices or exchange rates or interest rates are to be determined by various official and other exchanges, what controls must be in place? What should be the rules on ownership to prevent markets being rigged? In all cases, both the 'true' demand for and the supply of assets (goods and services) need to be examined carefully, and balanced within a long-term cost-effective framework.

4 Costs – what are the development costs (capital and revenue), ongoing operational costs, through-life costs (including maintenance and enhancements)?

5 Value for money and net added value – essential measurements in relation to investing in a new product or service. I invest now to achieve future benefits/returns. If I borrow to invest, I need to earn a profit above the interest rate I pay. Therefore what discount rate needs to be applied to relate current expenditure to future benefits and cash flows? A low internal rate of return implies that we are willing to forgo current benefits in return for long-term benefits, that there are not other more attractive investments, and that risks are minimal.

6 Funding – who is to pay? – via charges, taxation, borrowing, voluntary contributions, subsidies.

7 Management responsibilities and accountabilities for achieving the objectives and realizing the values, in relation to projects and to ongoing operations. Complex government initiatives led by ministers, via government departments, local authorities, public institutions and agencies, and involving consultants and private sector partners, seem too rarely to be able to provide proven value for money. Private initiatives also have a chequered history, but the disciplines of markets and competition drive good performance in the best-managed companies, both small and large. So, how is performance to be measured? What regulation of standards and performance needs to be in place? What governance is needed where and when?

8 Uncertainties – these comprise opportunities (included in and also beyond objectives) *and* risks (very often ignored or minimized by project sponsors, politicians and others with limited horizons). Short-termism is often rife in political and media circles. Complex projects and initiatives most often involve the impact and probability of future risks greatly outweighing the likely benefits of fresh opportunities.

9 Capabilities to achieve objectives. Many organizations, and notably government, have relatively short terms of office and employ general rather specific management capabilities to achieve results. Consequently they are most likely to fail to realize value since no one is truly accountable. All key roles should have clear definitions of the required capabilities for success. Our education systems should advance the development of the required capabilities. Beware of institutionalizing incapability. Focus on adding sustainable value.

Value

The following will be defined:

Core purpose

Objectives: what is to be provided, when, at what cost?

Beneficiaries: for whom?

Overarching values.

Defined measures of value.

Costs: all the related costs.

Funding: who pays, and how?

Provision: who institutes and who manages the ongoing provision?

What can be provided via the markets and what needs special provision?

What is the necessary and cost-effective value chain to meet each agreed requirement?

Uncertainties:

Opportunities: are there additional benefits to be realized?

Risks: what are the impacts and probabilities of occurrence of what can go wrong?

Performance measures: how do we measure success – realized net added values?

Controls: are additional measures needed to ensure safety, security, probity and legality? What governance is needed?

Calculations: how to sum up value. Added value arithmetic.

Introduction

02

Every significant thing done by us or for us depends on a decision on value – a value judgement, but hopefully much more considered than a personal opinion or prejudice. We should carefully define our overarching values so that these can be applied in ways that are mutually beneficial for our value chain partners. Value management should involve careful analysis and calculation. How much is something worth? Is this task worth the effort in relation to the likely outcome? What will other people or businesses be willing to pay for a product or service that I could provide? How much can I afford to pay my suppliers for good quality and service? These questions cannot be answered effectively until the value chain that is going to support the delivery of the final product or service has been defined, optimized and managed.

All too frequently the calculation on value is not done well. We and our 'masters' are not good enough at analysing the value to be added by a project or initiative or purchase or investment – our pension or savings plan, a house extension or overseas holiday home; or an NHS reorganization, or a transport plan, or a scheme to control immigration and population, or the provision of housing, or a military operation, or an energy investment....

This book aims to clarify the meanings of value, the role of overarching values, how to calculate net value and how to manage the realization of optimal added value. We shall show how to define and manage modern value chains which link all the key contributors to success. A value chain is the overall set of internal and external resources – human, physical, financial and informational – which require to be marshalled and managed in order to achieve cost-effectively the objectives of any organization.

Throughout this book, practical and theoretical insights into value chains shall be provided, to the benefit of key individual and collective decision-takers in the private, public, charitable and social sectors. The book also provides a framework to support students of many subjects – business management, government, philosophy, social anthropology, science and technology. We shall analyse some important value chains which matter to us all, in such a way as to encourage you to do the same for those key value chains you use.

With the support of the Chartered Institute of Logistics and Transport (CILT) we have constructed a 'website of value' to which all constructive contributions will be welcomed – **www.websiteofvalue.com**. Describe your value chain on it and share the questions you would like answered.

The meaning of a value depends on the item or service being bought or sold, on the end user and the decision-taker, on the buyer or seller, and on the supplier and funder. What is the objective of the transaction or project or initiative? Is it to enable something to be used or will it be a store of value?

Value is most often generated across a chain of linked customers and suppliers – individuals, businesses, farmers and raw materials suppliers, transporters, communications media, governments and institutions. Therefore there can be many aspects to delivering overall final value – there may be harmony or conflict, competition or collaboration, but the overall value chain needs to be understood and managed if best value is to be realized. Key factors in this include timing, geography and format – that is, time and place of delivery and use, and in what most useful form or forms.

In *The Wealth of Nations* (1776) Adam Smith wrote:

> Money has become the universal instrument of commerce by the intervention of which goods of all kinds are bought and sold or exchanged for one another. The rules which men naturally observe determine the relative or exchangeable value of goods. The word VALUE has two different meanings, and sometimes expresses the Utility of some particular object (Value in Use), and sometimes the Power of Purchasing other goods which the possession of that object conveys (Value in Exchange). The things which have the greatest value in use have frequently little or no value in exchange (eg water); and, on the contrary, those which have the greatest value in exchange have frequently little or no value in use (eg diamonds).

This argument still has great validity, even although Adam Smith was unaware of bottled water and industrial diamond uses. He clearly analysed the role of supply and demand in determining price and value within different markets. If I can cut costs of manufacture (eg via the division of labour and specialization), and thereby reduce prices, I can expand the market and thereby achieve further economies of scale. I add to my profits by bringing better-value products to the end user. I achieve a virtuous value cycle.

Optimizing value not only depends on the product or service and its price but also on when and where delivery takes place and with what degree of certainty. Optimum value arises when I can buy what I need at a price that seems fair to me and also receive delivery when and where I require, and also in an agreed format. Speed alone is insufficient. Speed and certainty must go hand in hand. Six bottles of wine ordered for a dinner party that will commence at 7pm are not equivalent to 12 half-bottles arriving at 10pm. Usually, the further away the benefit is expected to arrive after current expenditure, the less it is valued. If I invest money now to gain a profit in 10 years as opposed to five, I must discount the return each year for 10 years at an agreed rate of interest representing my opportunity cost (alternative investments) in order to determine what is my real net gain (or loss). Individual preferences in relation to place, time, format and certainty as well as price determine value; eg the value of water from the home tap as compared with in the desert with perhaps three days trek to the next oasis, and the values of diamonds at the Monte Carlo Film Festival as compared with a Saturday night dinner with friends at the local bistro, or when they have to be pawned (another type of liquidity).

David Livingstone (1813–1873), the great explorer, humanitarian and missionary, wrote in his diaries: 'No one knows the value of water till he is deprived of it... I have drunk water swarming with insects, thick with mud and putrid with rhinoceros urine and buffaloes' dung, and no stinted draughts of it either.'

Eduardo Porter, in *The Price of Everything: The cost of birth, the price of death, and the value of everything in between* (2011), writes: 'The poor choose among their options the same way the rich do, assessing the prices of their alternatives. The relative costs and benefits of the paths open to them determine the behaviour of the poorest Indian girl and the richest American man. These values are shaped by the opportunities they have and the constraints they face. The price we put on things – what we will trade for our lives or our refuse – says a lot about who we are.'[3]

Therefore, a democracy and an organization and an individual greatly benefit from a systematic framework for analysing value.

Here is an initial matrix for assessing value, which we shall develop and discuss in more detail throughout later chapters (Table 2.1). All of the following should be considered, to the varying degrees required, when evaluating a particular initiative, project, investment or action.

TABLE 2.1 Value analysis

For whom	Individual Owner User Investor	Community Inhabitant Visitor Supervisor	Society Citizen Child Deprived	Organization Business Charity Clinic	Government National Local Department
Objectives/ purpose	Consumption, income, capital, service provision, preservation (eg of environment – essential, desirable, luxury); a right (agreed basic or acquired), a merit/deserved, a privilege; freedom to do/from danger, hunger, etc; maximizing value/ minimizing loss/optimizing net added value				
Place/location	Where?				
Timing	When?				
Format	Tap/bottle, cooked/raw, personal/distant …				
Total demand	Elasticities of demand (how much will demand change as price or quality vary?)				
Value chain	Define key direct and indirect organizations for success. How to identify items and participants and to communicate relevant data securely between the key participants				
Cost	Capital, operational, through-life – direct and indirect costs				
Funding	Via revenue, taxation, borrowing, charitable sources				

TABLE 2.1 *Continued*

Charge	Full cost, average, marginal, subsidized, means-tested, free
Market	Local, national, international, open/restricted/monopoly, auction, flotation of shares
Liquidity	Timely ability to realize value
Provision	By state/government, agency, private, individual, voluntary
Total supply	Elasticities of supply in relation to price, profit (by how much will supply change as prices and margins alter?)
Balance of demand and supply	Degree of balance/imbalance at each key value chain stage – consequences
Uncertainties	Dependabilities – what are the margins of error, the known/unknown factors and data?
Opportunities	To add value, expand the market, secure supplies, improve safety and security – the positive aspects of uncertainty
Risks	Of losing value, making losses, product failures, penalties – the negative aspects of uncertainty. Risk assessment and mitigation; use of insurance, hedging, assignment of liabilities in contracts; the law of unintended consequences
Measures	Prices, profits, surpluses, service levels, customer satisfaction, queues, market futures, rates of interest (current and future – discounted cash flow/net present value)

Notes

1 Smith, A (1776) *An Inquiry into the Nature and Causes of the Wealth of Nations.*
2 Livingstone, D (1857) *Missionary Travels and Researches in South Africa*; (1865) *Narrative of an Expedition to the Zambezi and its Tributaries*; (1874) *The Last Journals of David Livingstone in Central Africa from 1865 to his Death*, Murray, London. In the parish church at Helmsley, Yorkshire, there is a fascinating letter from Livingstone to the wife of the Bishop of Cape Town, thanking her for sending him his first mosquito net – he died of malaria and other tropical diseases.
3 Porter, E (2011) *The Price of Everything: Solving the mystery of why we pay what we do*, Penguin.

Overarching values

03

Summary

Undertaking the development and management of a value chain will not bring satisfactory results unless you define meaningful values you wish to apply and also to bring into practice with your value chain partners. This is too important a task to leave to your Public Relations or Human Relations departments. Think it through and apply your sound overarching values both internally and across your value chain.

Giving life to values

Many organizations now publish their ethical values, such as concern for the environment, diversity of employees, fair trade, encouragement of smaller suppliers, and sustainability. When an organization genuinely has such values, they should be known to employees, shareholders, customers and suppliers, across their value chain. Nevertheless, many such values are relative rather than absolute – relative to the business, management, shareholders, charity, government, country, time and place. What does 'sustainable' mean – affordable by whom and how in the long term?

Are there fundamental values? 'Do unto others as you would have them do unto you' would seem to leave some ambiguity in relation to individual preferences. 'Turn the other cheek and do good to your enemies' would seem 'better' than 'an eye for an eye and a tooth for a tooth'. 'Love your neighbour' does not actually require you to like your neighbour, but rather to be concerned about and promote their welfare. Be a Good Samaritan.

This is not the book to delve into the realms of philosophy or theology – fools rush in where angels fear to tread.

I suggest that the most fundamental of values is to recognize the essential humanity which exists in individual human beings and to encourage that humanity, and not to neglect or extinguish it. The key concept in this context is 'care'. This has two fundamental aspects. I should genuinely care about others and also find the resources necessary to apply appropriate care for them well.

Do you care about your value chain partners – from consumers to customers to employees to direct and indirect suppliers? Do you care about the values of your value chain partners – what is a 'fair wage' in each supplier's country and do they pay it? How do they treat their employees and their suppliers? Does the degree of inequality between the remuneration of those at the top and those at the bottom matter?

Relative values

Where an organization has particular values which it intends to apply, these should be defined and communicated wherever appropriate across the relevant value chains. Where market forces are going to rule, this should be made clear. Adam Smith, whose profession was moral philosophy, explained that lower prices, and good quality, would increase the size of markets and enhance employment, each of which is supported by the division of labour and specialization, which in turn reduce prices and increase the market. Smith wrote: 'By directing that industry in such a manner as its produce may be of the greatest value, [the businessman] intends only his own gain, and he is in this, as in many other cases, led by an invisible hand to promote an end which was no part of his intention.' Also, businessmen 'seldom come together for merriment and diversion but that they conspire against the public good'. Hence a necessary role of government is to regulate or break monopolies. There is a perpetual dichotomy between people being encouraged both to be considerate of (care for) others and also to pursue their own self-interest, which may well benefit the majority as well as themselves.

In the modern world there is general agreement that all trades, professions and businesses should have defined standards of quality and performance, along with due balance between competition and monopolization. Some such standards are subject to legislation, notably in relation to safety (such as electrical wiring, food preparation) and accounting, competition and monopoly. Some are overseen by offices of regulation (Ofwat, Ofgen, Ofcom etc) with varying degrees of success (eg the media believe that they are worthy guardians of their own freedoms as well as ours); some have self-regulation (Law Society, Colleges of Medicine, Estate Agents and so on), which sometimes tends to favour the supplier rather than the customer.

Unfortunately, politics is a 'profession' where self-interest too often trumps ethics, let alone morality (eg sources and uses of funds). Legislation can help or hinder the generation of sound values but cannot provide them. The legal system is there to enforce and administer whatever the law requires, and therefore is necessary but not sufficient to instil appropriate values across society.

A critical area of disagreement about values relates to democracy and citizenship. Too often governments are unwilling to undertake the huge amount of time and effort required to understand why people respond in different ways to laws, incentives, rewards and punishments. If groups of people do not subscribe to the values promoted by the government, and do not feel part of society, trouble lies in store for them and for society. Values have to be transmitted wisely and systematically and sustainably – not something governments are good at.

Are immigrants aspiring to be British, and what does that imply? One of the best examples of creating a new culture of shared values was in 19th-century United States. Waves of immigrants went to the United States to escape from famine, persecution and discrimination, and also to seek better economic opportunities. Immigrant parents did not suddenly become Americans rather than Irish, Poles, Russians, Italians, Scots or English. But they wanted their children to be Americans, and to share a new language, without losing all sense of their origins. This was much more than multiculturalism. A key player in creating the new American set of values was William Holmes McGuffey, son of an immigrant from Scotland. In 1837 he published his first *McGuffey's Eclectic Reader* to teach sound English in the schools. By 1920 these readers had outsold (122 million copies each read by many pupils) all books except the Bible. McGuffey not only taught good English grammar and vocabulary. He also chose illustrative examples from the classic works of Greece, Rome and Britain and the Bible, which emphasized the importance of honesty, hard work, thrift, sobriety, modesty, conformity and overall morality.

Unfortunately, both McGuffey and Adam Smith were later 'purloined' by right-wing, conservative organizations, which adhered to different values. Unfortunately, the shared culture of the United States did not extend as far as the Native Americans.

A valuable conclusion

Think clearly and consistently about the values you wish to follow and the values you wish to be applied across your value chain, and indeed across society. Communicate and apply them in sustained and sustainable ways. Sound and appropriate values are vital prerequisites to realizing best value for you, your organization and your value chain partners. You are responsible. You choose.

Notes

1. Albert Schweitzer (the doctor, missionary, theologian, and organist) said in his great 1952 Nobel Peace Prize acceptance speech: 'Humanitarianism is the origin of all progress towards some form of higher existence. Inspired by humanitarianism we are true to ourselves and capable of creating. Inspired by a contrary spirit we are unfaithful to ourselves and fall prey to all manner of error.'
2. Adam Smith wrote the following in *The Theory of Moral Sentiments*. These echo my arguments for recognizing and encouraging a shared humanity and in seeking to care for others and to provide the means of care:
    a. 'How selfish soever man may be supposed, there are evidently some principles in his nature, which interest him in the fortune of others, and render their happiness to him, though he derives nothing from it except the pleasure of seeing it – behaving as if you are watched by an impartial spectator.'

b 'It is reason, principle, conscience, the inhabitant of the breast; the man within, (which is) the great judge and arbiter of our conduct. It is he who, whenever we are about to act as to affect the happiness of others, calls to us, with a voice capable of astonishing the most presumptuous of our passions, that we are but one of the multitude, in no respect better than any other in it; and that when we prefer ourselves so shamefully and so blindly to others, we become the proper objects of resentment, abhorrence and execration.' Note that there is a surprising resurgence, notably in the United States, about what Adam Smith wrote in relation to human values, for example *How Adam Smith Can Change your Life* by Russ Roberts and *On the Wealth of Nations* by P J O'Rourke.

3 The French philosopher André Comte-Sponville wrote *A Short Treatise on the Great Virtues* in 1996. How do we live a virtuous/good life? His virtues are politeness, fidelity, prudence, temperance, courage, justice, generosity, compassion, mercy, gratitude, humility, simplicity, tolerance, purity, gentleness, good faith, humour, love. I must reaffirm the virtue of care (I care and I shall employ the means of caring).

4 *The Gospel According to Luke*, translated from the Greek by William Barclay, 1968, Collins.

The optimal sequence of decisions

04

FIGURE 4.1 The 21st-century value chain

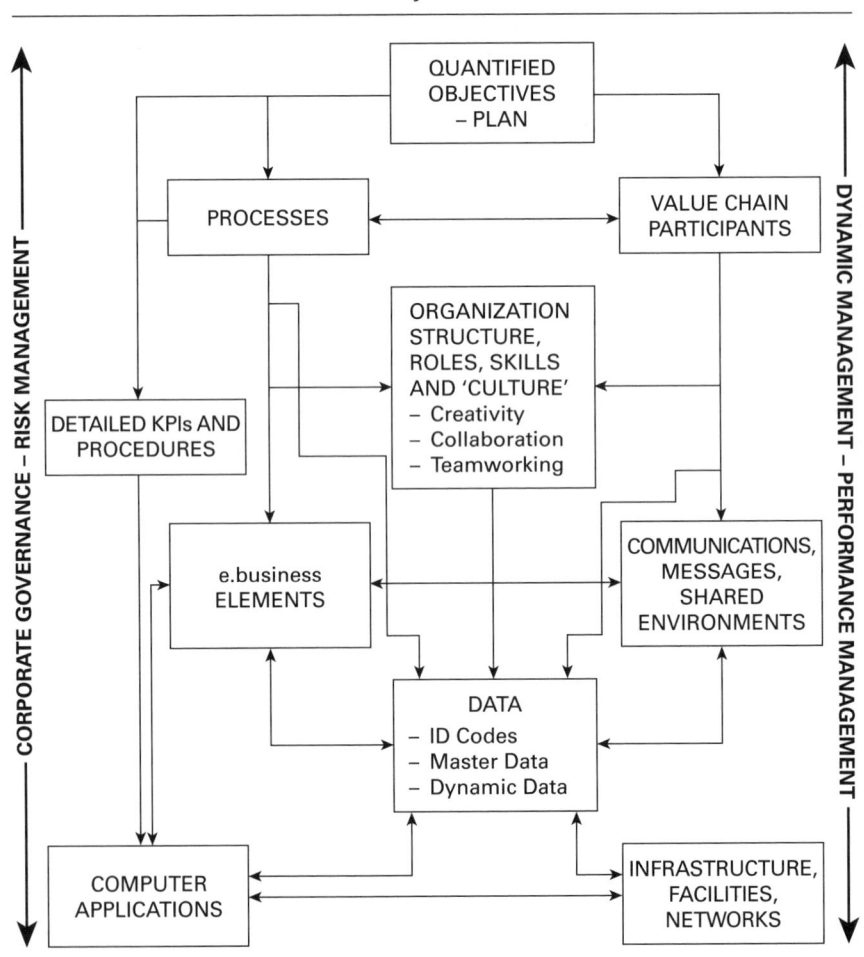

Summary

The sequence of decision-taking is vital for realizing best value and for effective value chain management. In Chapter 6 we review some modern value chains in terms of core purpose, strategy, objectives, plan, measures and targets, and issues. The first two of these, although important, are often described in a rather intangible manner. They are also often linked with even less rigorous titles such as 'Mission' and 'Vision'.

In this chapter, we assume that there is a core purpose and a reasonably coherent strategy for the organization. We also assume that there are agreed overarching values. Successful management of the organization and its value chains then depends on adhering to the following sequence of decision-taking:

1 Set quantified objectives: Review the current plan for achieving objectives.

2 Define the required value chain and associated processes.

3 Only then consider the required organization and supporting key performance indicators.

4 Design the value chain communications and supporting data.

5 Develop the communications network and the IT systems.

6 Agree a new comprehensive and integrated plan internally and externally.

The decision sequence

1 Quantify the objectives. These must be specific, quantifiable wherever practicable, measurable and time-specific, and not vague and general. Too often, inappropriate and unbalanced targets take the place of specific and realistic objectives and failure or ineffectiveness follows: eg a target to increase bank lending or cut immigration or for a patient to see a GP within 48 hours irrespective of the patient's real need. There must also be a rigorous and integrated plan to support the achievement of the objectives, and this topic is covered in Chapter 10.

2 Define the main business processes and associated value chains to support the achievement of these objectives – see Chapter 8. Processes run across value chains. Who are the key value chain partners and what are their objectives? Strategies are of limited value if they do not comprise clear objectives, well-defined processes with linked value chains, and structured and resourced plans.

3 Define the organization. Too often, a reorganization is instituted in order to try to achieve targets which are in fact sub-objectives (and too often sub-optimal), without fundamentally addressing the main processes. Key performance indicators, balanced targets and detailed procedures must link powerfully to both objectives and processes. The organizational culture is equally important. Understand the current social anthropology (tribes and customs, ritual languages/acronyms and 'dances') before deciding how best to change matters. Plans need to be translated into detailed and integrated actions, along with resources and responsibilities, across the internal and external value chains.

4 Re-examine the value chain communications across the organization and across the key value chain participants. At this stage, standard messages and electronic shared working environments need to be developed and supported by standard data elements, master data, identities and auto-IDs and dynamic databases – the data architecture to support the process architecture. See Chapter 8.

5 Computer applications can then be best defined. And last, the computing infrastructure, networks and facilities can be defined and implemented to support all of the above. Far too often, new computer systems are bought by management from companies and consultants in the vain belief that these will transform performance without having to do the hard work described above. No computer system will enable you to analyse and use your data effectively if you have not first structured your data according to the needs of your business and value chain.

6 Redevelop your business plan to incorporate the above in a clear and integrated manner.

Too often, reorganizations precede redefinition of processes. Worse still, computer systems and facilities may be defined in isolation from the necessary prerequisites, particularly processes, identities and data:

- Wherever practicable, employ evolutionary prototyping – get things right on a small, low-cost scale first before betting the business.
- Reiteration is essential within the above framework and sequence, and always related to the overall objectives.
- Uncertainties – opportunities and risks – need to be specified, quantified and mitigated within the business plan.
- A dynamic management system is needed, powerfully related to effective performance management, for which a sound data architecture is essential.

All the above needs to done within a sound framework of corporate governance and risk management. Current approaches to governance and to risk analysis and mitigation are too often unfit for purpose. See Chapter 11.

The value in value chain management

05

Summary

Here definitions are provided of the key value and value chain management concepts – net added value, net present value, earned value, value of a human life. In particular, the main measures are defined in order to support improved performance across the value chains – eg profit, costs, transfer prices, gross domestic product, end-user utility, service levels.

Definitions

The key objectives of any organization should be to optimize net value (NV) to the end user at a low total cost and also to optimize net added value (NAV) to each of the intermediate participants in the value chain. Value means utility (value in use, the benefit derived). Therefore the particular focus of value chain management (VCM) is to determine how utility to the end user can be both enhanced and delivered cost-effectively.

In everyday commercial activities, value is most often measured by price (value in exchange) – value chain partners buy and sell. Value also relates to the charge incurred, or the cost of provision. However, additional measures of utility are also required where there is no price, or where utility and value bear no direct relationship to cost. Further research and development are needed in relation to defining value added, notably from the perspectives of the end users, consumers, citizens and taxpayers. While the price paid (or cost incurred) for a product or service will tend to reflect the balance between supply and demand at a particular time and place and within a certain timescale, it can often not reflect ongoing value to many of the key stakeholders – for example, a footballer's transfer fee, a chief executive's total remuneration package, a trader's bonuses, a political lobbyist's financial contribution, an MP's expenses and so on.

Hence there is often no single agreed measure of value. Several measures may need to be used in order to provide a meaningful picture and to make realistic comparisons. Thus, gross domestic product (GDP) tries to measure the value of each nation's annual output. However, there is substantial disagreement about what to include in GDP (the latest additions to it are, for example, prostitution services and illegal substances – they have a positive value/price but a negative value/utility to society). GDP does not measure the quality of life, the degree of fulfilment the citizens can expect, the value of the natural and physical environment, nor the expected ongoing utility of current output and investment to future citizens. Equally, the health of a nation cannot be measured merely by longevity. See Diane Coyle on GDP: 'There is no such entity as GDP out there in the real world waiting to be measured by economists. It is an abstract idea and one that after half a century of international discussion and standard setting has become extremely complicated.'[1]

VCM differs from other approaches to management by rigorously reviewing objectives, processes (human, physical, financial and informational) and uncertainties (opportunities for improvement and risks to achievement) from beginning to end of the chain in an integrated manner, across all key stakeholders, in order to optimize agreed overall value and its key components.

Value can often be measured by what someone is willing to pay for a product or service because of its utility. However, the price should reflect the estimated future stream of benefits from the item or asset being bought, that is, its 'fundamental' value. NAV at each stage in a value chain and also overall often means the difference between price (or charge) and cost (capital, operating, direct and indirect costs); that is, the revenue from sale less the cost of production, most often the profit. The price of something is usually determined by balancing supply (determined by its availability and cost and by competition) and demand (determined by its utility and available funds and by competition) within a defined timescale. For example, water is invaluable. It is a necessity. But its price will be determined by demand and supply, not only generally in each region of the world, but seasonally, daily and by location. Thus, the marginal cost of a glass of water out of the tap in a British home is zero; the average cost to the consumer is the annual consumption divided by the water bill; the price of a bottle of chilled water on a boat sailing on salt water in summer is high, but it will be bought if the personal utility exceeds the price and the funds are available, and if total demand does not exceed supply.

Utility is determined by performance and timeliness – will a product or service meet a need when required? Performance, in turn, is composed of output, outcomes, throughput and also quality and reliability.

Value is greatly affected by uncertainty (opportunity and risk). Thus, lack of confidence in a currency causes its value (exchange rate) to decline, and a general lack of confidence in currencies causes the price of other value stores, such as gold (which has limited practical utility), to increase. Valuing a product or service in a currency depends on the currency's price (rate of exchange with other currencies), which in turn depends on the complex interactions of demand and supply for all the items being traded in each currency, including speculation and hedging. A good friend once made his fortune by trading in cargoes of oil from the Middle East. He would buy and sell 250,000 tonnes of oil several times between the Arabian Gulf and, say, Rotterdam and at the same time endeavour to hedge against currency fluctuations. He retired early, wisely and successfully.

Valuation is therefore often difficult. Uncertainty in any value chain causes costs to rise since steps need to be taken to provide physical or financial 'insurance'.

Value is added over a period of time. Cost too is incurred over a period of time, and total or through-life cost takes much longer to appear. It may be incurred not only by the immediate supplier, but by third parties and by society, for example the costs of health, education, transport or pollution.

How to do more with less – frugal innovation

A great deal of imaginative thought has recently been applied to how to improve the value delivered to the end user and also to the value chain (VC) participants by learning from and with people in developing countries about how to improve productivity in 'simple' ways. Employ the imagination and practicality of those who have to be cost-effective in order to survive. Link them into the value chain through the spread of mobile phones and the greater availability of local credit and of inexpensive payment mechanisms. Many examples are given by Navi Radjou and Jaideep Prabhu in *Frugal Innovation: How to do more with less*.[2]

Value chain linkages and interactions

It is difficult, though essential, to try to measure the effect of a substantial change at one stage in a value chain on the other stages and participants. Employing Keynesian language, an investment at one stage will have multiplier and accelerator effects on others. Individual and business propensities and decisions on how much to spend and on what, and on how much to save and how, need to be modelled as well as is practicable, particularly under conditions of great uncertainty.

Value chain management measures

The stated purpose of VCM is to deliver the greatest utility to the end user by optimizing the NV to him or her, and also the NAV for each of the value chain participants. The chain can be a 'simple' physical supply chain; or it can be a complex human, physical, financial and informational network interlinking the public and private sectors internationally; or it can be a patient-care 'pathway'. VCM is concerned with all the components required to achieve the objectives, and it takes a holistic view of all processes and participants. 'Success' is easier to measure where there is a price and a profit. However, many services, public or charitable, or functions within a business, have no price, but only a cost and, one trusts, a value or utility. Therefore VCM must also concern itself with the cost-effectiveness by which agreed objectives are achieved. VCM also uses cost–benefit analysis to compare tangible and intangible benefits with the costs of providing them. Value for money analysis attempts to compare different ways of achieving the same end through cost–benefit analysis – which way will produce best value for money? Other related terms are value analysis and value engineering.[3]

Valuing human life

Often values are implied. Thus, what is the value of a human life? Various parties take very different and often inadequately defined and perhaps conflicting views of this: for example, a court of law determining compensation; the NHS determining whether a treatment is to be made available at all; a doctor determining whether a particular individual will receive that treatment; a patient believing that his life is worth preserving because he has paid his taxes all his life; the Armed Forces in battle – our soldiers' lives in comparison with enemy soldiers and with civilians' lives; or a religious denomination's definition of the sanctity of a co-religionist's human life. It is important that the valuation of a human life should be done explicitly whenever practicable.

Where price and cost are inappropriate measures of utility or value, subjective or ordinal measures may need to be used. For example, there could be two alternative ways to help people. One could be twice as effective as the other but take four times as long to help the same number of people. Approach A might have utility U and help 1,000 people in the same time that approach B with utility 2U would help 250 people.

The respective utilities could then be valued in the ratio 1,000U : 500U = 2 : 1.

Stocks and flows

Improving NV to the end user and NAV to the value chain participant often involves focusing on stocks and flows. Generally, stocks should be relatively low and flows should be relatively fast. The objective is to achieve agreed speedy *and* certain service levels at a low total cost. The total costs of production and distribution capacities need to be considered (including balanced capacity utilization). Thus inventory needs to be sufficient to meet an agreed level of service and at the same time prevent a loss of sales (or of life) or excessive production and distribution costs. Inventory usually costs substantially more than the annual interest on its book value when costs of storage and management, waste and write-offs, are taken into account (say 25 per cent rather than 10 per cent cost of capital). Thus, determining optimal stocks, flows and capacities is a vital, though complex, part of VCM.

A variety of measures of VCM performance are given at the end of this chapter. Measures need to be appropriate to the particular value chain, and where necessary may be 'soft' as well as 'hard'.

Net present value

Since both benefits and costs arise over periods of time, a technique is needed to value these on a consistent basis. Cash (value) flows are discounted to their net present value (NPV) at agreed rates of interest, which in turn are often determined by the opportunity cost of capital (what would the funds earn elsewhere?). While NPV and discounted cash flow (DCF) are relatively straightforward to use in most of the private sector, they are more difficult to apply in social and political situations. It is easy to work out whether a warehouse should be rented or bought given an agreed rate of interest and a confirmed view on the desired payback period. It is much more difficult to compare the benefits and costs to all parties of, for example, not importing products from developing countries now in order to prevent that carbon footprint from damaging their land and livelihood in 10 to

100 years' time. What is the trade-off between people suffering a loss of income or starvation now, so that any survivors can have a 'better' life in 20 or 50 years' time? Although there are no easy answers, more sound and public calculations of real utility are needed. Assumptions should be made explicit.

It is inevitable that different people, different organizations and different governments will often use substantially different discount factors when comparing present versus future costs and benefits.

Furthermore, it is rare to find proponents of strong views on global topics (such as climate change, globalization, fair versus free trade, organic farming, nuclear power, renewable energy, biofuels) explicitly calculating how many people at what levels of value the application of each policy would support, and how the winners could compensate the losers at agreed levels. This brings us back to the importance of defining clear and sound objectives and of the sound design and management of the supporting value chain.

Earned value management

This technique (EVM) is used to assess the progress made to date on a project in relation to the costs already incurred, and thereby to forecast what still needs to be done, what it will cost and how long it will take. However, little real value is realized until a project is completed, and there is a tendency (especially in IT projects) for the 'last 10 per cent' of a project to take 90 per cent of the time. Nevertheless, EVM is a 'valuable' technique, recognizing that value in this context means the cost of work satisfactorily completed – see Section 15A.2, Reference 9.

The estimate of valuable work done to date in relation to time taken measures the rate of progress. This is a guide to the time it will take to complete the work. However, ongoing calculations must be made on what risks remain and what efficiencies will be achieved in the ensuing stages.

Costs incurred to date in relation to work done (and to the budget) measures both current cost-effectiveness and possible future costs, when related to revised estimates of work still to be done.

Transfer prices

These usually relate to the charges made by one value chain participant to another where both have a common owner, and particularly where they are operating in different countries. Hence transfer prices are not usually determined by market forces. When transfer prices are set too low, they discourage the supplier, and vice versa. Therefore setting the value of an optimal transfer price is an art as well as a science (eg in relation to minimizing the total international tax bill), in order to avoid the effects of the law of unintended consequences.

Conclusions on value

Be as clear as is practicable on how value and utility are going to be defined and measured in your world. Where necessary, use two or more balanced measures of value, such as the cost of a medical treatment allied to the extension to the patient's economic and social life. Focus on enhancing utility and value at each stage in a value chain and for the end user. Be clear on who are the value chain participants and end users. Ask them what adds and what destroys value. Analyse prices, charges and costs (and especially through-life costs), along with expected forward streams of benefits from investments, in order to optimize net added value across the VC, and hence net value to the end user. Model alternative scenarios. Agree the rates of interest to be used to relate present and future costs and benefits, investments and net ongoing returns, from the standpoints of the key stakeholders, including those who pay and those who benefit.

VCM endeavours to improve the value of the total cake without necessarily deciding how the cake should be shared among the VC participants. Collaboration among the participants should be judiciously employed in order to enhance value in ways that do not damage necessary and legal competition – see Chapter 9. Often competition must be left to do its best, although within a wise frame of governance.

Notes

1 Coyle D, *GDP: A brief but affectionate history* (2014), Princeton University Press
2 Radjou N and Prabhu J, *Frugal Innovation: How to do more with less* (2015), The Economist, London
3 See also Chapter 15 references.

A review of some modern value chains

6A

FINANCE | FOOD | AUTOMOTIVE | ELECTRONICS

6A.1 The financial value chain

Core purpose

To support the development, production, distribution and sale of and payment for goods and services through the provision of funds at acceptable costs.

To link savers with borrowers in order that:

- Savers are willing to lend money to the banks and other financial institutions in the confidence that they will earn an acceptable return and that their investments are safe.
- Borrowers have access to funds at acceptable costs and for appropriate periods of time.

To link those wishing to buy and sell currencies, commodities and other investments immediately, and also at specified future times at fixed prices – forward buying and selling ('hedging').

Note that the financial value chain includes commercial banks, investment banks, merchant banks, private banks, insurance companies, building societies, pension funds, investment trusts, hedge funds, currency and commodity exchanges, stock exchanges, central banks and other national and regional regulators, including state treasuries, the European Central Bank, the International Monetary Fund and the World Bank.

Strategy

To attract both lenders to support the advances to borrowers and also shareholders to provide the base capital to support the ongoing business. Depending on the financial institution, the demand and supply markets for funds will vary in relation to the opportunities for profit and the risks to be undertaken and the degrees of liquidity. Each institution will seek to use its own borrowings, and multiples thereof, to make investments in loans to borrowers and also in attractive opportunities such as company shares, property and commodities, including currencies. A financial institution dealing with the general public and with smaller enterprises should be more 'conservative'/risk-averse in its borrowing and lending than one operating globally in diverse markets and currencies. Nevertheless, all financial institutions should be very much risk aware (see Chapter 11 on managing uncertainty).

Objectives

To provide acceptable returns to shareholders and thereby to attract and retain their funds.

To meet the needs of many categories of customers, both lenders and borrowers, traders, insurers and the insured and even 'speculators'.

To satisfy financial regulators in each country of operation and globally. This is not necessarily easy to ascertain since, for example, there is disagreement about the definition of base capital and reserves and about the effect that various such levels will have on the ability to operate cost-effectively. Regulators also disagree on how far the different types of banking activity should be kept distinct, for example high street commercial banking and global investment banking.

To attract and retain staff with the requisite capabilities within a sound system of incentives.

To develop and manage a rigorous and effective governance framework.

Plan

There requires to be an appropriate integrated and comprehensive set of plans covering all operations and defined time horizons. Too often financial intermediaries have allowed individuals to make impressive (but temporary) returns in new high-risk areas of activity without effective planning or governance. Too often financial intermediaries have extended their operations beyond the limits indicated by their base capital and agreed reserves.

Measures of performance

Returns on capital employed; profit margins per type of business; debt and lending volumes in relation to base capital and agreed reserves, as agreed with regulatory bodies; market shares; share values; cost ratios per type of business; volumes of lending per type of customer; bad debts; fines from regulators; staff turnover.

Issues

The financial crises of 2005 to 2010 and beyond resulted in the (near?) meltdown of much of the world's financial and economic systems. It is evident that almost all participants in the financial value chain had a very inadequate understanding of at least three fundamental factors:

1. The nature of the financial value chain (FVC) – that is, who or what adds (or can destroy) what net value, by what means, at each stage in the chain, from the first lender to the ultimate user of the funds. There is no final real product of the FVC – it is, or should be, a mechanism for supporting the development, production, distribution, sale and payment for real goods and services, by linking savers with borrowers, and in particular with those who create real economic wealth and value. In value chain management, the key participants are the customer (in this case the borrower; but in other VCs the buyer) and the supplier (in this case the lender or saver, together with the

investor and with investments; but in other VCs, the seller). These participants are in a network of relationships with individuals (such as citizens and employees), agents (such as banks, insurance companies, moneylenders and cash and document transporters) and authorities (such as central banks, government treasuries and other regulatory bodies) – see Chapter 8 on constructing sound value chain process and data architectures. Modern FVCs are very complex since the participants, products and processes keep changing (at least in name). Defining a rigorous audit path across multiple pathways, organizations, markets and countries is often very difficult, and this makes modern FVCs difficult to map, measure, predict and control. This may be the reason why FVCs have not been well understood nor managed; but this is no excuse.

2 The uncertainties and the constituent opportunities and, even more importantly, the constituent risks present at each stage in the value chain. The greater the complexity, the greater the uncertainty, and the greater the risks for many involved in the financial value chain. Furthermore, complex mathematics has been increasingly applied, resulting more in superficial sophistication than in genuine benefits to FVC participants. Too many of the opportunities that arise within this complexity are available to only a small number of insiders. The fundamental value of a financial asset is the stream of net benefits it is expected to yield over its lifetime. The market value of an asset is what someone is willing to pay for it at a particular point of time. The greater the uncertainty about the relationship between these two values, the riskier it becomes to pay the market price, other than for short-term speculation. Diagnosis of the economic past is much more accurate than prediction of the financial future. As JK Galbraith remarked in *The Economics of Innocent Fraud*: 'In the economic and especially the financial world, prediction of the unknown and the unknowable is a cherished and often well-rewarded occupation... The men and women so engaged believe and

are believed by others to have knowledge of the unknown; research is thought to create such knowledge. Because what is predicted is what others wish to hear and what they wish to profit from, hope or need covers reality.'

3 The need for effective governance – this is a substantial problem in both banks and their regulators. For example, it was reported in the *Financial Times* in October 2015 that only 6 per cent of directors overseeing the world's biggest banks have any technology experience, in spite of such key issues as IT failures, digital challenges, cyber insecurity and the increasing complexity of mathematical algorithms for trading.

Analysis

A bank makes money by lending multiples of its base capital plus its deposits. So long as the borrowers repay their loans on time, plus interest reflecting their particular levels of risk, there is confidence in the bank's liquidity.

In theory, the prices that investors and their agents pay for financial assets, given free and fair competition, will represent reasonable balances between supply and demand. In practice, fools (the ignorant, unwary or greedy) and their money are always too easily parted. Information about prospects, options, charges and risks is limited for most investors, and short-term speculators have very limited interest in developing longer-term real value for the economy. However, it is the supply of real goods and services that generates the ongoing returns (value) which enable an economy to grow soundly in the medium to long terms. That is, businesses borrow money to invest in fixed or working capital, or to support their cash flows, and they add to total economic value by generating more revenue than costs. Out of this profit they pay interest on their loans, various charges to advisers and dividends on their share capital, generate retained earnings to grow their operations and pay taxes to support the state.

A simple financial value chain is:

Lender → Bank → Borrower → Bank → Lender

together with any investments of available cash made by the bank in equities, property and other assets in order to enhance returns.

The uncertainties facing lenders and banks mainly relate to which particular businesses or individuals (borrowers), and which financial institutions (agents), will do well or badly. Further uncertainty may come from key national and international factors, such as national bank rates, rates of inflation, exchange rates, rates of economic growth, and taxation and tariffs. Outcomes in this 'simple' world depend on the balance between the demand for, and the supply of, funds.

Figure 6A.1 illustrates, simplistically, the complex financial value chain of banks and other financial institutions. Such institutions not only link savers to borrowers, but also lend to and borrow from each other, as well as linking with a wide variety of financial institutions such as hedge funds and private equity groups.

FIGURE 6A.1 Financial value chain: simplistic map of complexity

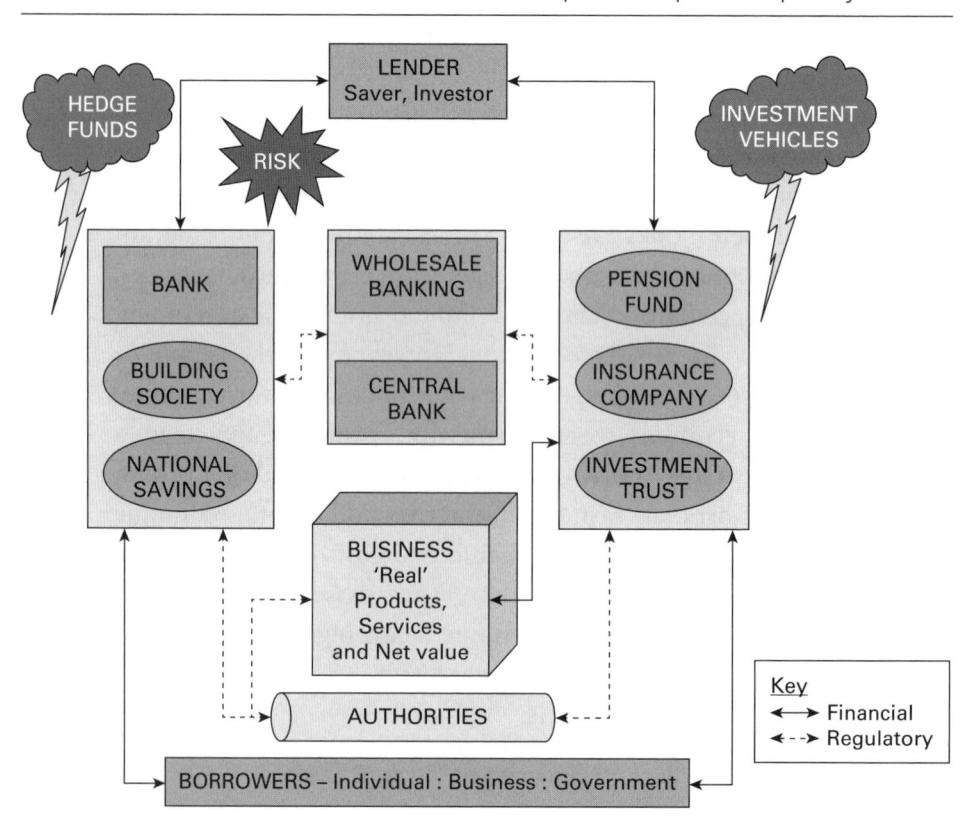

In 2008/9 I wrote in *Value Chain Management* (p 21):

> The simple concept of the Central Bank Rate becomes overshadowed by LIBOR (The British Bankers' Associations' London Interbank Offered Rate). This is the most important interest rate in the world, covering possibly $300 trillion of contracts, equal to $45,000 per human being. LIBOR is the real set of 150 interest rates fixed daily, which governs interbank lending including interest-rate swaps, along with mortgage rates and other loans to individuals and businesses.

It became evident that many of the traders' activities around the setting of the LIBOR interbank rates had only a little to do with determining sound interest rates and much to do with making money for the dealers and their employers on the turn.

Subsequently it emerged that certain individuals in key banks were colluding in order to establish LIBOR positions that would enable them to realize hundreds of millions of pounds and dollars. As reported in the *Financial Times* in May 2015, a trader wrote in an e-mail subsequently evidenced by the US FBI: 'If you ain't cheating you ain't trying.'

It was also discovered that similar collusions were going on in the foreign exchange (FOREX) markets and in other financial marketplaces. Banks and other financial institutions have been fined many billions of dollars, pounds and euros by the regulators. The US FBI said that criminality was on a massive scale. Nearly all the massive fines have been levied on the guilty financial institutions (and hence on their shareholders). Only in 2015 was the first trader sent to prison for illegal trading – it is unclear how far his employers turned a blind eye to his activities, which were making him and them vast sums of money. Risking the shareholders' and the customers' money was worthwhile to the traders and their employers because they believed that they had little to lose personally. The rest of us paid their bills in higher bank charges in total and for such transactions as currency exchanges. How could any sensible person believe that a few individuals and institutions could be making billions of pounds, dollars and euros by manipulating FVCs without other people, businesses and countries paying the bill in higher charges and lower returns? Furthermore, this has resulted in less funding being available for legitimate business investment such as by small to medium sized companies.

Other examples of the growing problems in financial markets include 'flash crashes', where prices of commodities gyrate dramatically over a short period of time, for example in oil, energy, metals and exchange traded funds. These rapid fluctuations in prices are engendered by complex mathematical algorithms manipulated by traders in order to gain relatively small margins many times over.

It is remarkably difficult for most investors to determine what levels of risk are implicit, rather than explicit, in many investments, especially when these are in such bodies as hedge funds, currency and commodity funds and in financial organizations that invest in these and similar parts of the FVC. It is equally difficult to discover what these investments are costing in total. Attempts are being made by financial regulators to clarify 'acceptable behaviour' by financial institutions and to introduce much more effective audits, reporting and governance.

Much remains to be done by national and international regulators to define the financial value chains that should exist, and to prevent those that potentially diminish net value for the value chain users. It is essential that we the people can see clearly the nature of each FVC.

In this complex financial world, loans and debt can be packaged in order to disguise their contents from the unwary. The same financial instruments are sold and resold, without adding real value, but greatly increasing real cost. The gearing or leverage of debt to real equity can be beyond reason or wisdom. For example, if investors place their savings with a hedge fund, venture capital group or similar financial vehicle, the money earned by investing their funds in other businesses' equities may earn, say, 6 per cent. But, 4 per cent of this can 'disappear' in the form of the intermediary vehicle's directors' fees, fees to other investment banks, trading costs and management fees. Real value is not generated merely because these sums are then spent in the real economy on goods and services, nor because this activity generates some tax revenue for the government. Governments should not acquiesce with FVC activities that diminish benefits to the 'real' economy simply because they generate tax revenues to the Treasury. The word 'hedge' should be restricted to a transaction that reduces risk for the lender, or for the buyer of a commodity.

Secondary trading, involving the sale and resale of equities and other financial instruments, also adds costs (profits to the intermediaries) without benefiting the original investor. In 1965 the annual turnover of UK equities as a percentage of GDP was 10 per cent. In 2004 it was 200 per cent. Momentum trading, for example, focuses on exaggerating upward market movements and exiting downward trends early, for example by shorting. Such actions by traders lead to much greater uncertainty (it is estimated to increase market volatility 15 to 20 times), and certainly to greater risk to the original investor. While outstanding equity values in the United States in September 2008 were valued at $40 trillion, derivative instruments based on these were valued at $1,000 trillion. Hedge funds, for example, got 2 per cent of the annual value of the 'assets' they 'managed', *plus* 20 per cent of each short-term 'profit' or gain, *plus* a percentage of any tax breaks. In 2014 it emerged that the real total charges to pension funds by investment intermediaries are several times greater than hitherto believed. Short-term financial 'ducking and diving' by the traders on the inside of markets is not longer-term hedging against risk for the 'normal' investor, since hedging means agreeing to a financial contract that aims to reduce risk, for example hedging against fluctuations in exchange rates or commodity prices.

The administrators of the collapsed Lehman Brothers and other undisciplined financial intermediaries faced huge difficulties in unwinding the assets and liabilities involved in dealing with hedge funds and other parties through 'billions of bilateral, over-the-counter trades outstanding with hundreds of counterparties'. It is believed that settling the main issues in relation to Lehman Brothers' affairs took around three years. Unravelling all the complexities took a decade and involved several hundred million dollars in audit fees.

Few investors, or even conventional banks, building societies, pension funds and insurance companies, fully understood these financial value chains and their constituent instruments, or what they were being charged. When instruments such as collateralized debt obligations (CDOs) appeared, involving a mixture of prime and sub-prime mortgages, or other dubious debt, fewer still understood what they were buying and the inherent risks. Governance was substantially inadequate. Lloyd Blankfein, the CEO of Goldman Sachs, was reported in the

Financial Times as saying that: 'We let the growth and complexity in new instruments outstrip their economic and social utility as well as the operational capacity to manage them.'

Good value

Until February 2015, it seemed like a good idea to quote from *Good Value: Reflections on money, morality and an uncertain world*. What more apposite title could there be in relation to the book you are now reading? *Good Value* was written by Stephen Green, former CEO and Chairman of HSBC, and both an Anglican minister and a government minister. *Good Value* was a *Financial Times* Book of the Year in 2009. The *Wall Street Journal* wrote: 'At a time when bankers are being pilloried for bringing about a global economic meltdown, this is an unusual and thoughtful disquisition on how to conduct oneself in a world of high finance and ambition, in, as he puts it, the global bazaar.'

Rev Lord Green was, for some time, responsible for the Swiss private banking arm of HSBC. This assisted many rich people to reduce greatly what might/should have been due in tax.

Conclusion

We have a long way to go before the financial value chain operates with a dependable certainty, morality and cost-effectiveness focused on the end user. It requires much more effective internal and external governance. The FVC must operate well and predictably in order to serve the legitimate needs of each citizen, business and country. Much remains to be done nationally and internationally to achieve such predictable value for all.

Proposals

In order to ensure that real value is being added in the longer term, and to ensure that effective governance is being exercised, it is essential that:

1. Each financial value chain is clearly mapped, in order to indicate each participant and its role, its relationships and its contribution to net fundamental value (or disbenefit).

2 The volume of each key type of activity (eg buying and selling of equity, debts, options to buy and sell, shorting), and the ratios of volume to capital, or to equity, and gearing and leverage ratios, are clearly shown, along with safe limits. Financial techniques that add no value to the end user, and those that may destroy much value, should be severely constrained or prohibited. Individuals found guilty of breaching the rules should be personally punished, rather than just the financial institution and its shareholders.

3 Uncertainties (opportunities and also risks) are specifically predicted, that is, impacts on end users (borrowers, lenders and shareholders) multiplied by probabilities of occurrence, in relation to both the supply of and demand for funds. Thus, for example, if an option to buy is sold to another party, what are the risk trigger points and how much is at risk at each level? Indeed, should selling options to buy be allowed, particularly when shares and rights are being borrowed temporarily from other businesses rather than owned? Selling an option to buy is gambling that the price will fall, and borrowing rights in order to drive the price down is 'nobbling the horses'.

If one cannot map and evaluate the value chain, its components, tools, roles, benefits and costs, risks as well as opportunities, do not invest – unless of course you enjoy gambling, you have vetted the runners, and you trust the bookmaker.

6A.2 The food value chain

Core purpose

- Providing value for money.
- To meet consumer needs for nutritional and enjoyable foods at affordable prices, while supporting the levels of revenue and profit that will motivate each participant to provide ongoing acceptable availability, quality, safety, service and environmental sustainability.

Strategy

- Develop a value chain which has quality, variety, speed, certainty, safety, security and sustainability at an ongoing low total cost.

- Develop a good consumer and purchaser franchise by the execution of excellent innovation, product development, marketing and advertising, value for money, production and service. Recognize that the buyer of food may well not be the sole consumer of what is purchased.

- Establish sound nutritional standards with consumer and regulatory bodies and encourage their adoption.

- Meet the needs of consumers in all socio-economic groups at the times and places where they choose to purchase and to eat. Innovate in order to satisfy and also to shape consumer requirements

- Support the development of high-quality supplies from dependable suppliers.

Objectives

- To develop, produce and distribute profitable, competitive, differentiated products, in terms of taste, branding, value for money and availability.

- To maintain high levels of food safety and quality through managing the entire value chain. To institute effective controls and measures of performance at each key link in the value chain.

- To achieve consumer awareness, distribution and display, and thereby profitable market share.

- To capture reliable data on consumer needs, attitudes and use of communication and distribution channels. To undertake sound market research and product testing with consumers.

- To ensure so far as is practicable that key producers and suppliers remain profitable and dependably in business and that they can support necessary research and development.

- To stimulate fresh sources of supply, notably in developing countries, recognizing that food crops are susceptible to climate, disease, conflicts and other uncertainties and risks.
- To reduce waste in relation to both production and consumption.

Plan

- Balances demand and supply cost-effectively at each key stage in the value chain at appropriate time intervals. Quantifies all important elements of income and expenditure.
- Defines the detailed activities, resources and responsibilities for each stage of research, development, marketing and sales, procurement, production, storage and distribution, consumption and waste disposal. The plan of each business function must be integrated within a total plan so that each function is directed to contribute well to overall business and value chain objectives.
- Defines how risks to quality, safety and continuity of supply are to be identified, quantified and mitigated.
- Defines how required revenue, profit and market share are to be achieved.
- Defines exploratory R&D, including nutrition, ingredients, biochemistry and allergies.
- Defines collaborative activities with customers and suppliers across the value chain.

Measures/targets/KPIs

- Consumer health and nutritional standards (difficult to define, and to assign responsibilities, eg being obese or overweight).
- Profitability of all players in the chain, plus ROCE. Profit and cost margins per product category.
- Customer and supplier service levels that relate to both certainty and speed. These are critical in the fast-moving consumer goods (FMCG) industry, which includes food. These

also relate to inventory levels, which need to satisfy product availability objectives as well as 'lean' and 'agile' supply chain management principles.

- Number of stock-keeping units (SKUs). Manufacturing, storage and distribution costs escalate with the number of SKUs. On the other hand, more SKUs may be needed to meet the requirements of particular market segments.
- Market shares.
- Investments in R&D.
- Satisfactory shareholder returns.
- Meeting environmental and political targets, which may be complex and are often conflicting – eg health and well-being, anti-obesity, additive-free, free of gluten or milk, good shelf life, climate change, organic, fair trade, free trade, ethical, genetically modified (GM) or not, local production, minimal but secure and sound packaging, minimal waste, safe, protectionist, animal welfare, farmers' incomes.

Analysis

The food value chain includes farmers, fishermen, cooperatives, middlemen, seed suppliers, processors, commodity markets and exchanges, brokers, speculators, transporters, agribusiness including fertilizers and pesticides, governments and their agencies (pro consumer and pro farmer, health and safety etc), development agencies, R&D institutions, design agencies, marketing and advertising agencies, communications media, intermediate manufacturers, packaging, printing, finished product manufacturers, packers, logistics services, wholesalers, retailers, farmers' markets, caterers, cooks, personal and home shoppers and of course purchasers/consumers/eaters.

Food products must be safe and protected. Packaging is expected to be identifiable, transportable, secure/tamper-proof, descriptive, as well as attractive and brand reinforcing, biodegradable and at an acceptable cost – and also minimalist. Tricky to achieve.

No value chain can meet all the needs and expectations of all these participants. Therefore, objectives, processes and data across the value chains need to be made more explicit, and realistic trade-offs require to be calculated. Competition and collaboration need to be balanced. Brands need sound protection, but 'protectionism' needs to be avoided except where it is necessary to allow a potentially viable product to be brought to market locally and globally. Dumping of surplus foodstuffs resulting from subsidized farming in developed markets into developing economies is 'immoral'. Charity and development aid need to be differentiated from each other. Without adequate local legal protection, effective quality standards and a reliable, safe and cost-effective distribution system, developing countries will be unable to provide acceptable quality, prices and service to potential markets. They need dependable access to developed markets in order to develop.

While branding and some ingredients may well be global, it is often the case that food consumer tastes and reactions are local, as are systems of distribution. Therefore product and packaging variations are substantial. Value chain complexities can be considerable; but sound value chain management helps to optimize these cost-effectively.

Major changes continue to take place across the food supply chain, notably from competitive forces – discount retailers, overseas competition, home shopping and delivery, click and collect, social media and consumer comments online, cheaper 'Value' product ranges, pressure on consumer incomes and on business profit margins (which may lead to reductions in quality).

There is a growing potential to link the food and health value chains electronically. As more people wear or carry apparel and devices that can provide continuous monitoring of health and/or need for nutrition or drugs, signals can be sent to both the individual and the clinician to take prompt action.

The retail food value chain

Within the food value chain a major retailer has been selected for an analysis against the overall value chain. All organizations have their own procedures, languages and indeed social anthropologies (tribes and customs). These can serve an organization well by setting understandable and motivational objectives; but they have to be understood within the context of the total value chains, and they must evolve accordingly. For example, the food industry is very competitive. While total expenditure by consumers on food varies in relation to disposable incomes, the variety of products and prices that 'need' to be offered, the increasing competition among retailers and the extra costs of providing new services such as home shopping result in declining profitability for all. Sales may well rise while profit margins fall.

I give below this retailer's own words, and then comment in relation to the food value chain.

Retailer core purpose

'Create value for customers to earn their lifetime loyalty' (but consumers never give their lifetime loyalty. Such loyalty as there is usually relates to a well-known brand rather than to a particular retailer. Medium- and longer-term loyalty has to be earned and re-earned. Consumers may be becoming less loyal, as both alternative supply channels and communications media increase in number).

Goals

- 'To be a growth business' (depends on consumer disposable income and priorities, and on the shopper's view on relative value for money across all their spending options. Growing sales volumes may well result in diminishing profit margins).
- 'To become the business people value more than any other' (somewhat unrealistic; depends on what competitors do and on consumer reactions. The stock market also has an ever-changing view of the value of businesses).
- 'To have the most loyal and committed staff' (people do like to work for successful businesses, especially where they share in the profits. Sound business processes and effective training, together with management that is good at both execution and communication, greatly help commitment).

- 'To be a global retailer' (depends on individual markets and on the timescales – needs to achieve adequate profitability. Few retailers achieve this objective, since one approach rarely fits all in global retailing).
- 'To be as strong in non food as in food' (this is difficult since each consumer market requires substantially different attributes. Food is unlike finance is unlike fashion).

Strategy

- UK is the core business.
- Non food is to be developed.
- International business is to be expanded.
- Retailing services are to be added, eg personal finance, telecoms.

This has stayed almost unchanged since 1995 (all staff were very familiar with it. However, external and internal events have resulted in major changes of direction).

Each objective has an ARCI

(This is one retailer's management acronym and it is a good one – other companies have variants.)

- Accountable – only one person who owns it.
- Responsible – those who carry it out.
- Consult – those who must be consulted before change.
- Inform – those who only need to be advised of change.

Shared plans

These include all stakeholder needs – customers, staff, management, investors and key value chain partners. Each part of the physical supply chain has a set of plans, from stores to warehouses.

All are aligned

Targets are (ideally) 'BRAG' reporting (this is one company's acronym):

- Balanced (B): outperforming, but may possibly cause a significant problem elsewhere in the chain.

- Timely (R): needs corrective action.
- Realistic (A): caution, there may be a problem.
- Achievable (G): on track.
- Simply communicated: these letters are applied to performance against each target.

(Note that other companies use various management acronyms, the most common being SWAT – strengths, weaknesses, opportunities and threats. Some companies use red, yellow, green or numeric scales, such as 1–5.)

The analysis illustrates a key issue facing the true evaluation of the total food value chain. Each major UK retailer (and manufacturer) may be performing well and have implemented the core purpose, strategy, objectives, plan and measures within their own 'value chain' to its individual satisfaction. When, however, we look to the core purpose of the total food chain, the objective of satisfying each key participant and especially the consumer is not necessarily being met. There is always a fundamental dichotomy in competitive marketplaces between what best supports consumer needs and what sustains individual business profitability. For example, providing a home shopping service is often necessary for competitive reasons but it rarely improves profit margins – it adds to the total costs of distribution. Few companies, including the retailer illustrated, continue on their intended growth paths without some major traumas (such as the 'horse meat scandal' – when meat processors in Eastern Europe 'unwittingly' introduced horse meat into supplies to Western Europe – or other ingredient 'scares'). Too many companies have employed overly optimistic financial reporting in order to boost share prices and executive remuneration. The best companies make it a 'hanging' offence to bring earnings forward from the next year or to delay costs into the next financial year.

Since it is impossible (and unwise) to plan and manage the food value chain centrally, market forces have to be allowed to operate, but within a wise regulatory framework encompassing food safety, operational safety, fair competition, governance and dependable reporting.

In the area of food production there is much debate about global vs local sourcing, use of 'sustainable products', distortion of the market by government/regional subsidies and so on. The ongoing World Trade Organization rounds of talks illustrate that in many cases parochial pressures take precedence over overall food value chain management, which aims to bring most benefit to the final consumer while also satisfying the key participants.

Having said all the above, the quality of the food industry, its value chain and its managements is high, since it is difficult to succeed and easy to fail. Risks are great and complexities are considerable. Food companies understand, own and manage their risks very well, since serious failures could occur anywhere in the value chain. Remember that the food industry could kill more people than the defence and health industries combined, if it did not take its responsibilities so seriously.

6A.3 The automotive value chain

Core purpose

Car manufacturers aim to gain the lifetime (that word again) loyalty of customers by delivering high-quality cars that customers want and can afford. Manufacturers must also sustain the resale value of those cars throughout their lifecycles via the provision of a comprehensive after-sales service and repair network. Providing customers with vehicles they enjoy involves designing and managing complex worldwide value chains.

Strategy

Manufacturers offer dramatically different options to their customers. Some offer limited product variety, and largely sell from stock. Others look to offer a wide selection of modular product variety, and aim to deliver this through building cars to customer order. According to the lean supply chain principle of 'runners, repeaters, strangers', popular specifications can be produced for stock (runners), including showroom and demonstrator cars. The less frequently ordered but common specification mix (repeaters) is delivered through amending existing orders in the order pipeline (this is also commonly known as 'build and amend'). Finally, the majority of seldom-ordered models (strangers), which is a low proportion of actual sales, are supplied via completely new customer orders added to the production programme.

The after-sales service supply chains offered by manufacturers operate separately from the new car supply chain. However, these are managed on the same principle of 'runners, repeaters, strangers' – items are managed through 'category demand analysis and periodic review', where central management of inventory aims constantly to re-evaluate demand and to maintain availability. Fast-moving, commonly required parts are held at or near franchise dealers and their related but independent repairers. The slower-moving, less frequently required items are often held in national or regional warehouses and delivered according to the urgency of the order. The very long Pareto tail of slower-moving products is often held in central global or regional warehouses. This long tail of slower-moving items includes a proportion that are stocked for over 20 years after a model has ceased production, in order to meet the requirements of customer loyalty and product lifecycles.

Objectives

- Sustained profitability that will satisfy shareholders and also enable R&D for new models and features.
- Market shares in established and also new geographical, fashion and technology markets.
- Repeat purchases from individual, corporate and fleet purchasers.
- Securing maintenance expenditure from customers on an ongoing basis.
- Accurate, relevant and up-to-date information shared across the value chain participants.
- All the above has to be done in close collaboration with the sales and repair dealer network, much if not most of which is under separate ownership.

- Meeting evolving national and international standards for quality, safety, economy and emissions.

Plans

These need to be highly developed, integrated and costed across the various value chains. They must include contingency plans to cover any failures of supply, which could disrupt production and thereby customer service. Marketing plans must be well integrated in order to stimulate demand when it can be well satisfied.

Measures

- Customer satisfaction with the product. Reliability is key – mean times between component failures. Causes of failures.
- Market shares for each segment.
- Profitability of all partners in the value chain, plus ROCE and returns to shareholders. Therefore also share prices.
- Service levels to customers and from suppliers.
- Component costs.
- Inventory levels of finished products, components and spares.
- Efficiency and environmental standards – by size of engine, type of fuel, nature of emission. In 2015 major problems appeared with the particle emission and fuel consumption standards set by the authorities in various countries as well as with the accuracy of the results being achieved by certain vehicle manufacturers.

The factory supplier value chain

Component suppliers are based all over the world, although there are concentrations in the home countries and continents of the manufacturers. Speed and certainty of supply are essential, along with dependable quality and low cost. A supplier must be very reliable when modern production lines depend on each activity stage often taking as little as one minute before the production line moves forward. Parts must be available when required, supported by preceding quality tests.

In addition, new methods of production and new materials are continually being developed. For example, the 3D printing of components is being introduced, as are super-strong and light materials such as graphene. Furthermore, countries that previously imported most of their cars and components are now increasingly able to manufacture or assemble these themselves. The automotive value chain is ever-changing.

Retuning the current value chain

Given an uncertain global economy, every manufacturer is looking to reduce inventories and to cut any excess stock of unsold cars. The stock in the supply chain includes stock at franchised dealers, market stock in compounds and stock in transit on rail, road and sea. For a volume manufacturer with a European market share of around 5 per cent, the value of total stock of finished cars in the market is estimated at around €1.2 billion, with every additional day's sales' worth of finished vehicle stock in the supply chain estimated at €20 million. These values are based upon normal operations, but dramatic falls in demand place an extra stress on these supply chains. The tied capital and the cost of funding unsold stock are major causes for concern for all carmakers. Therefore, rigorously amending planned production and generating completely new orders are both a priority for car makers.

Different manufacturers run different systems, but essentially the car supply chain involves dealers searching for cars that meet the selection criteria given to them by the customer. More sophisticated search mechanisms enable a search of all dealer stock, central stock, stock in transit, and planned and amendable orders in the order pipeline. The more flexible manufacturers have an amendment cut-off date closer to the day of scheduled production. However, a key aspect of being able to offer high product variety based on modular platforms is being able to search for a match to an existing, amendable or new order, and thereby give the customer a reliable delivery date based on their product preference; that is, certainty as well as speed.

High-end luxury value chain

Most brands with a high level of build and amend to customer order do so out of the 'luxury' afforded to lead-time by a specialist product. The more prestigious the marque, the longer customers are generally prepared to wait for the product. However, a premium European carmaker decided that it needed to increase the reliability of its search and order booking system. A key bottleneck from the customer perspective was the delay between a product specification request entered by a salesperson with a customer and receiving a dependable response. If accurate data delivered via sound information systems are viewed as fundamental components of value chains, delays in the systems can be considered a critical waste. Delay means that an order query is wasting time, delivering out-of-date information and so creating inordinate instability and uncertainty for both the value chain and particularly the customer.

Therefore, the carmaker embarked on replacing the ordering systems used in each market by the franchised dealers and national sales companies (independent importers or market-based carmaker sales subsidiaries). The new improved order search and booking system is shown in Figure 6A.2.

Generating and fulfilling orders with speed and certainty

The key aspect of the new ordering system detailed above is the ability to check the availability and delivery date before the order is confirmed, a feature that can provide the customer with useful information during the sales discussion. The new ordering system tagged customers to orders in final assembly to allow for order swaps and possible build-date issues.

The search and booking system required the integration of several batch-process-driven legacy computer systems. The new system was designed to be flexible enough for adaptation to different market requirements while ensuring that nothing compromised the integrity of the central process. Crucially, not only were the intended users at each stage in the supply chain integrated from an early stage, but the

FIGURE 6A.2 The new improved order search and booking system

Customer	Dealer	NSC/Importer	Carmaker	Plant	Suppliers
Create configuration					
	Check sales marketing, existing stock				
	Create order				
		Check delivery pipeline			
			Check order pipeline		
			Check technical specifications for build		
				Check possible production slots	
				Check production constraints	
					Check key component supply
				Place order in pipeline	
			Calculate delivery date		
		Check contingent operations			
	Check financing				
Confirmed delivery date					

support teams, which would manage the IT performance after handover, were also brought in early in the design process in order to enable them to learn about and contribute to systems during their development.

Communication, internal marketing and training were critical to the successful adoption of the programme, which required the participation of both manufacturing and all the sales markets. The system was rolled out to pilot markets and integrated into the pilot plant and first-tier suppliers over a period of 18 months, after months of consultation, planning and design. The latency (or delay) in handling the order query based on entering a specification into the configuration and search mechanism was reduced to around five seconds, much the same as online airline booking systems.

The ordering system has now been successfully deployed across markets and plants, and it provides a reliable and leading-edge order-to-delivery production system. The success of the implementation was made possible by a shared agreement across the value chain that the new system was central to achieving the business's core objectives. This belief was made crystal clear through total commitment at top managerial levels, including board-level project involvement. Such end-to-end value chain capability, which also includes effective links through to component suppliers, cannot protect a carmaker from turbulence in the marketplace; but it can help in delivering a lean, low-cost and responsive automotive order-to-delivery system, providing exactly what the customer wants when required.

Issues

It is evident that all countries and economies depend on passenger and goods vehicles to a huge extent, and will continue to do so 'forever'. It is vital that vehicles are safe, economic and environmentally acceptable. Individuals need to be free to travel but within a framework that minimizes damage or danger to others. Much more sound research needs to be done on future fuels and fuel economy and total fuel costs, on safety and also on emissions and their measurement and control. We must be able to trust not only the vehicle manufacturers, retailers and repairers but also the standards bodies and inspectors who specify and then verify that we get what we need and expect.

6A.4 The electronics value chain

This includes hardware and software designers (in data processing, software embedded in complex equipment, in communications media, electronic games and many other areas); product design; raw materials suppliers; semiconductor manufacturers; original equipment manufacturers (OEM); hardware manufacturers; brokers; transporters; governments and their agencies, including physical and cyber security and defence; development agencies; R&D institutions; advertising and marketing agencies; packaging and printing; finished product manufacturers; packers; logistics services; wholesalers; retailers; consumers. All industries are supported by the electronics value chain in some way.

Core purpose

To meet consumer and industry requirements for electronics, while supporting the levels of revenue and profit that will motivate each participant to provide ongoing acceptable quality, safety, service and environmental sustainability. To provide essential software that is both dependable and imaginative.

Strategy

- Develop a value chain that has creativity, speed, certainty, safety, security and sustainability at an ongoing low total cost.
- Develop a sound electronic product marketplace by the execution of excellent innovation and cost-effective implementation of both end-products and their means of production, supportive software, marketing and service.
- Meet the ongoing needs of both industry and consumers.
- Support the development of high-quality components from dependable suppliers.

Objectives

- To develop, produce and distribute profitable, differentiated end-products and also components to be incorporated elsewhere, in terms of functionality, suitability for mass production, aesthetics, fashionable appeal, branding, value for money and availability. This includes spares.

- To develop the essential supportive software.
- To maintain high levels of product safety and quality through managing the entire value chain.
- To achieve consumer and industry awareness, distribution and display, and thereby profitable market share.

Plan

- Defines the detailed activities, resources and responsibilities for each stage of research, development, design in product, software and marketing terms, production, distribution and usage and waste disposal.
- Defines the current and likely future markets, timescales, market shares and competitive activity.
- Defines how risks to quality and safety are to be identified, quantified and mitigated.
- Defines how required revenue, profit and market share are to be achieved.
- Defines necessary R&D. This includes ongoing technological and scientific invention and innovation in relation to both hardware and software.
- Defines collaborative activities with customers and suppliers.

Measures/targets/KPIs

- Product satisfaction and reliability.
- Profitability of all players in the chain, plus ROCE, total sales, market share, customer and supplier service, cost product control.
- Satisfactory shareholder returns.
- Meeting environmental and political targets, which may be complex and even conflicting – eg efficiency, fair, ethical, local, packaging, waste, safe in relation to both use and to raw materials and chemicals and their disposal, copyright protection.

Analysis

Within the sector, initial product investment costs can be very high (for example, semiconductor companies firms tend to have very high fixed costs). Therefore, coherent value chain and management plans and processes are vital. The relatively short life of many electronic products and their software also requires these value chains be both lean and agile. One further issue for consideration is that providing spares and support for short-lived products can be expensive. The other side of this coin is that complex products such as aero engines need to be supported over many years across the entire globe.

The greatest usage of semiconductors is within data processing, communications, consumer products and transportation. The electronics sector is extremely significant in that its products and/or components underpin every other industry as component parts of products or processes. Computers are utilized in virtually every home, business, organization and government. At a consumer level, the demand for electronic products is ever-increasing, with most individuals becoming more technology aware. On the other hand, it is often technological development (ie the supply side) which stimulates or even creates demand. Fashion can sometimes be more important than need. And fashion is fickle.

In 2015 Apple became the largest, most profitable and most cash-rich company in the world. According to the *Financial Times*, in May 2015 the top four global brands were Apple, Google, Microsoft and IBM. On the other hand, several well-known competitors who in the recent past had been market leaders are 'struggling'. It is tough at the top of electronics and computing.

The product lifecycle is reducing, with an emphasis on providing new and innovative products to the marketplace at great pace, with older technologies becoming obsolete in a relatively short time. Competition and collaboration therefore need to be balanced. While some products, components and software within the sector are commodities, others require significant levels of development investment and will need high levels of collaboration and joint working across the supplier network for both product development and the provision of integrated manufacturing and assembly processes. There can be a risk of counterfeit products within the value chain, so the necessary controls need to be in place across the value chain to mitigate this risk. Developing countries already provide significant manufacturing input to this marketplace with substantial product cost benefits.

Restriction of Hazardous Substances and Waste Electrical and Electronic Equipment (WEEE) directives also affect companies in the electronics sector. Along with the obvious implication of managing hazardous substances, distributors must take financial responsibility for the sound environmental collection, treatment, recovery, recycling and disposal of an equivalent amount of WEEE to that which they produce.

Electronic products must be safe and protected. Packaging is expected to be identifiable, transportable, secure/tamper-proof and descriptive, as well as attractive and brand reinforcing, biodegradable and at an acceptable cost. Brands, and most products, are global. However, there are occasions when local variations (including instructions for use in each language) are needed. Consumer instructions in many languages can run to pages of print. Too often instructions that were clear in the original language become confusing in translation. Both product specifications and packaging may vary for some branded items, thereby adding to cost and complexity in the value chain.

The electronics value chain is evolving quickly and in many new directions. It needs to be well designed, mapped and managed to benefit us all. Watch this space.

A review of some modern value chains

6B

PUBLIC SECTOR | HEALTH | DEFENCE EQUIPMENT | PUBLIC TRANSPORT | WATER

6B.1 The public sector value chain

This section should be read in conjunction with Chapter 6C, 'Reform of the government value chain'.

Core purpose

To provide products and services, paid for by taxes and levies, agreed by Parliament to be needed by society, which the citizens are unable or unwilling to provide for themselves.

Strategy

- Government ministers and politicians propose initiatives to Parliament, or take actions.
- Senior civil servants write policies and advise on potential issues and on likely costs and also draft legislation.
- Government departments, agencies and private and voluntary sectors implement.

Objectives

To make a country:

- wealthier
- better educated
- safer
- healthier
- more competitive
- socially and environmentally attractive
- and also more law abiding
- and many more.

Plan

Many short-, medium- and longer-term plans. Too often, public sector plans lack rigour and integration. Politically attractive policies do not necessarily result in structured and cost-effective plans.

Measures/targets/KPIs

Numerous:

- Gross domestic product (GDP) per head.
- Percentage of university graduates, percentage achieving each school standard.
- Percentage employed and unemployed.
- Life expectancy.
- Percentage below 'poverty line', however defined.
- Numbers in jail. Crime levels.
- Numbers of immigrants, which can be analysed in terms of likely permanence, asylum seekers, economic migrants, students, EU and non-EU, wealthy individuals.
- Government borrowing as percentage of GDP.
- Balance of trade and balance of payments.
- Numbers of foreign visitors.

Issues

Issues relate to:

- Which products and services should the state provide, to whom, and which should be privately funded and/or supplied? What should be the size of the public sector? To what extent should people fend for themselves?
- What should be the burden of taxation, what charges should be made by the state, and on whom should these fall?
- How can the ever-growing needs and expectations of citizens be met within an acceptable tax base, and thereby how can much greater cost-effectiveness be achieved?
- How can wealth creation be encouraged sustainably, at home and abroad?

A fundamental issue is the failure by governments, local and national, to define clearly the outcomes they realistically intend to deliver. The following are examples of lack of clarity and obfuscation: good health and care for all; comprehensive and affordable public transport; universal and effective education for all; fair and transparent taxation; visible and effective policing; decent housing and so on.

Too often, initiatives are short-term and reactive, inadequately considered, over-complex, beyond the capabilities of existing staff, badly and expensively implemented and with unintended consequences. Nevertheless, we all depend on government to work predictably and well. We all have a major interest in the public sector value chain operating better. To be fair, we often say that we are displeased with some aspects of the public sector but that we prefer ours to many of the alternatives.

Objectives are rarely specific, quantified and realistic, especially within a politician's speech or political party manifesto. The arithmetic is often poorly done. The value chains, processes and data necessary to support their achievement are too rarely defined well and thought-through.

Planning of both operations and major projects is insufficiently realistic, quantified, integrated and inclusive of uncertainty and risk analysis, and also of how effective management is to be undertaken. It is wrongly believed that the risks inherent in projects and initiatives can and should be transferred to private sector suppliers. Furthermore, it is unrealistic to believe that the voluntary and charitable sectors will fill the gaps left by the public sector universally and consistently.

There are too many targets, which are often ill-considered and unbalanced. Great care needs to be taken to understand the capabilities, the motivations and also the constraints and limitations of staff, before demanding the moon. Continuity in post is often inadequate. The social anthropology of each of the very many tribes must be taken into account. These matters are analysed further in Chapter 6C on reforming the government value chain. I lay great emphasis on the governmental value chain because it underpins and greatly affects all other value chains. It is necessary, though not sufficient, for all to succeed.

Analysis and proposals

- Politicians are too often unlikely to have had experience in designing, developing, planning and managing substantial businesses, projects or value chains.
- There is a tendency to look for headline-grabbing initiatives and short-term results, and to have more, and more complex, initiatives than could reasonably be expected to succeed.
- Senior civil servant capabilities do not tend to be in the areas of achieving outcomes cost-effectively, nor of reducing complexity to match the capabilities of their staff, nor in defining sound process and data architectures.
- Enhanced training in value chain management is vital. Public sector selection and training need reforming.
- Consultants and business people brought in to assist are understandably often driven by the profit motive, which is not what drives the public sector.
- Training of public sector staff tends to emphasize 'soft' skills (eg health and safety, team building, sustainability, diversity) at the expense of outcome-focused 'hard' skills (such as rigorous definitions of benefits and costs, and of risks and their mitigation, plus project management).

- Capabilities are insufficiently tailored to job content. Time in post at the higher levels is often too short to achieve complex outcomes.
- Penalties for failure are inadequate, often because accountabilities are unclear.
- Following procedures can be viewed as more important than achieving outcomes.
- There is need for a new cadre of management, with the capabilities appropriate to successful public sector value chain management:
  - capable of defining more sound objectives;
  - undertaking rigorous cost–benefit analyses;
  - developing and running simpler, standard, speedy, certain, secure and low-cost value chains and related process and data architectures;
  - developing new public sector agencies with sound organizations and cultures. These agencies would be given longer-term objectives, funding and appropriate resources.

  This cadre is in addition to politicians and their advisers and senior civil servants. But, it is instead of much of the current government departments (and also their use of consultants). All the public sector need a much better understanding of uncertainty (opportunity and risk) and thereby how to define and manage complex projects (notably those involving IT).

- Sound process and data architectures must precede IT systems, as must evolutionary prototyping (get it right on a small scale first).
- Given sound objectives, processes, data, organizations and cultures, allied to longer-term resourcing and funding, public sector cost-effectiveness can be increased substantially over time.

Example

It was unrealistic to expect the weakest part of the NHS, the Primary Care Trusts (PCTs), to balance the books while driving up performance, in managing the increasingly 'independent' and 'competitive' bodies (eg Foundation Trusts) which make up the extremely complex health value chain, by exhorting the PCTs to achieve 'world-class commissioning'. Unrealistic expectations have now been put upon GPs (local doctors) and CCGs – see Chapter 6B.2, 'Health and care value chains'. This reorganization cost billions of pounds and has achieved little.

Priorities for value chain management in the public sector

Financial planning, management and control; project management; operations management; health and care, and social services; benefits and welfare; energy; housing; legal system; defence; Home Office; Revenue & Customs; transport; education; IT; governance and regulation.

6B.2 Health and care value chains

Core purpose

To return people with health problems as soon as is practicable to their communities to live and work well by means of cost-effective treatments and support. To care for those who are not capable of caring for themselves, temporarily or permanently, and who are agreed to need support from society and/or the state.

Strategy

To provide a broad series of physical and mental health and care services in relation to prevention, diagnosis, treatment and aftercare by a variety of means – mainly public but sometimes private, or semi-independent (eg GPs) or voluntary, up to the nationally determined level of funding.

Objectives

Require clarifying. It is very difficult, but vital, to define clearly what is meant by health and by care. There can be confusion between saying that certain treatments and services will be provided and then 'proving' that these will result in the required standards of health and care, that is, agreed outcomes. There is a tendency to have targets rather than realistic, specified, balanced and consistent objectives. Focus should increasingly be on outcomes, especially from the standpoint of the individual.

It is not always easy to set objectives for preventative medicine. However, the flu vaccine helps to minimize outbreaks of influenza and the MMR vaccine has greatly reduced the incidences of measles, mumps and rubella.

A major issue is the tendency of government ministers to promise that all needs will be met without defining total costs and timescales. However, in practice, not overspending annual budgets is a key objective. Under-spending or mis-spending is usually less of a sin.

When politically set objectives are not realized there is a tendency to assume that 'reorganization' or 'incentives' or 'competition' will succeed where lack of sound objectives, cost-effective processes, relevant and timely data and capable management have failed, or not been tried.

We now need to redefine the value of health and care services, and to set sound, realistic objectives for the whole of society. What services should we realistically and affordably deliver to whom, where and when and how?

Plan

There are many national and local plans, but inadequate integration. Tendency to avoid formally integrating demand and supply either nationally or locally.

Measures/targets/KPIs

- Time to obtain a GP appointment, but linked to limited time available to GP with patient and to GP surgery opening hours.
- Time to hospital admission, but linked to hospital waiting lists.
- Waiting times for cancer and other major diseases, diagnoses and treatments.

- Accident and Emergency 'maximum' wait, but confusion on when the waiting actually starts and finishes, and what constitutes actually being in A&E. This is related to trying to reduce the numbers using A&E, for example waiting in ambulances or on trolleys in corridors, to avoid triggering the wait time. Note that treatment that takes place within one hour of arrival is more effective on average.

- Dealing effectively with major accidents and disasters.

- Diagnostic test times.

- Time to deal with complaints.

- Difficulty of measuring outcomes from patient's standpoint. From the patient's standpoint, successful outcomes are far more important than the number of treatments performed per surgeon/per department.

- Failure to define and implement satisfactory and consistent performance standards for hospitals, clinics, GPs, consultants. For example, the best consultants will not necessarily have the 'best' results since they will undertake the most difficult procedures

The National Health Service (NHS) ranks in the middle of European Health Services in terms of outcomes but relatively well in terms of total costs as a percentage of GDP. Private health facilities and care homes vary widely in quality and in financial viability. It is not evident that the US health system provides value for money even for those who can access it. It provides some of the best medical treatment in the world, but it can appear to operate significantly for the benefit of the medical profession, private hospitals and insurance companies rather than the patient unless they are well-off or not often unwell – improved care for the US poor or uninsurable is sorely needed.

In the UK, the NHS is both a political football and a hot potato. There are endless reorganizations, even when these are promised not to happen. It is difficult to remember an effective Secretary of State for Health. It is difficult to remember even who the Department of Health Permanent Secretaries have been. Leaders of the NHS have often been more noted for their political than their managerial skills.

Mental health services remain the poor relation of physical health services. Unfortunately, many mentally ill people end up in prison or remain on the streets. Some mental illness (notably schizophrenia) can result from the use of cannabis and some other drugs during the teenage years. Substantial prevention of mental illness can come from the early diagnosis and treatment of behavioural problems in young children. However, in many parts of the country, mental health services cannot cope with the growing demand, which can come from GPs, Social Services, the police and from individuals and families. While a psychiatrist may just have enough time to provide a sound diagnosis and ameliorative medication, sustained improvement often requires the support of a clinical psychologist and ongoing nursing and community care. These are in very short supply in many parts of the country. The best clinicians believe that structured encouragement (instead of enforced compliance) of patients is vital to improving their mental health. Thus, to what extent do mentally ill persons choose to break the law and thereby end up in prison? How best can they be encouraged to progress well within society?

In relation to care services, there is even less clarity and a major lack of data. We have little accurate information on the numbers of the elderly with each key requirement for care. Co-ordination of care services for the old (and the young) is limited. The situation is made worse by central government giving local government many responsibilities for care but steadily eroding the available funds. Some major private care home companies are now in great financial difficulty. Bed blocking occurs in hospitals when the elderly have no adequate care resources available to them.

Few older people and few of limited education, with complex needs or requiring aftercare, can navigate their ways through the labyrinthine pathways without substantial support. I spend many hours helping the elderly to communicate effectively with the right people in the NHS, local government, care organizations, GPs, district nurses, pharmacies, public utilities and banks. This work includes translating confusing letters, telephone calls and completing complex forms. Quite often, for example, the failure to attend an appointment comes from the patient not understanding what is required of them (in addition to other patients not bothering to attend).

There needs to be a substantial reassessment of what should constitute cost-effective and integrated health and care value chains from the standpoint of the end user, as well as the health professional, the taxpayer and the government. Substantially more money will need to be spent to provide effective care for the elderly. If this is not well-planned great sums will be spent by default. Better care could be provided at an agreed total cost via the application of modern effective value chain management.

NHS value chain

The NHS is the largest state-funded health service in the world, serving over 90 per cent of the population who have not chosen private healthcare. It employs about 380,000 nurses, 150,000 doctors, 160,000 other professional staff and 37,000 managers (see **www.nhs.uk**). The NHS spends over £100 billion per annum.

Core principles

These were established in 1948:

- Meets the needs of everyone.
- Is free at the point of need.
- Is based on a patient's clinical need, not ability to pay.

These have more recently been amplified:

- Aspires to the highest standards of excellence and professionalism.
- Aspires to put patients at the heart of everything it does.
- Works across organizational boundaries and in partnership with other organizations in the interest of patients, local communities and the wider population.
- Committed to providing the best value for taxpayer's money and the most effective, fair and sustainable use of finite resources.

Strategy

Providing facilities, funds and skilled resources appropriate to each type of health and care need and to each main region. Endeavouring to win the confidence of users by providing timely and effective treatment and care. Anticipating requirements through research, selection and training of requisite staff and cost-effective collaboration with suppliers throughout the world (eg pharmaceuticals and equipment). Managing very large and complex value chains well.

However, strategy can vary:

- By year depending on political and social priorities (eg role of 'commissioning' versus 'providing' – which organizations should commission/order health and care services and which provide them – should any group do both?). This balance varies over time.
- By clinical preferences. However, sound national practice recommendations are well made by the National Institute for Health and Care Excellence (NICE). In a sense, a recommended medical pathway is a form of value chain.
- By area/post code (eg local funding, resources and facilities, or even in relation to arbitrary deficits or surpluses).
- By moving funds between organizations: CCGs, Foundation Trusts, NHS England (see also NHS Scotland, NHS Wales and NHS Northern Ireland), regional and national bodies, local authorities, government departments (eg medical treatment of soldiers and convicts).
- By the availability and cohesion of local authority and voluntary care resources.
- By condition (eg dentistry, eyesight, hearing, physiotherapy and mental health are not funded to the same extent as physical health).
- By age of patient.
- By what use should be made of the private sector and who should decide this aspect of strategy: the government, the clinicians, NHS management? What do 'privatization' and introducing 'competition' actually mean?
- Strategy has included Foundation Trust status for better performing hospitals and other facilities in order to improve financial discipline by giving such trusts more independence and responsibility. In practice this makes it more difficult to

provide consistent and integrated health services since the funding of Foundation Trusts in relation to other bodies can be inconsistent.

- Attempts have been made to improve the allocation of funds according to need and according to work done. However, the funding of PCTs and now of CCGs is a riddle wrapped in an enigma. PCT funding was done via an incredibly complex formula with over 50 factors which still managed to exclude some key ones, such as the number of very old people in an area. Meanwhile the Payment by Results scheme, which funded acute hospitals to which patients are referred by GPs, was more of a 'Payment by Activity', ie hospitals are often paid per treatment they actually undertake, whether or not commissioned by a GP, and whether or not having a successful outcome. In an area with a large percentage of retired people, who used to be relatively well-off and healthy, and with a relatively large number of GPs, together with 'active' hospitals, there was and is an almost inevitable financial deficit. Industrial areas with supposedly disadvantaged populations and relatively fewer doctors almost always generated financial surpluses. I believe that I am one of the few people who have tried to understand the complexities (including logarithmic indices of morbidity) of NHS funding in relation to NHS expenditure. Deficits (and occasional surpluses) continue to appear within many NHS bodies without satisfactory explanation and resolution, other than by writing them off.

- The use of IT in health has great potential (for making available accurate patient records, for linking treatments to outcomes, for online expert diagnoses and even treatments) but has had limited success, usually in certain diagnoses and treatments. Huge initiatives such as Connecting for Health have been expensive failures. Evolutionary prototyping has rarely been used in order to eliminate bugs and enhance performance on a small scale before going for broke. GP systems have often been varied and incompatible with central systems. I argue later that understanding the relevance and accuracy of data must precede the application of technology – Chapters 7 and 8.

Objectives

The NHS aims to provide a comprehensive service open to all, via the highest standards of professionalism and care.

As the complexities of the health and care value chain grow, along with ongoing advances in healthcare, objectives need to be wisely reassessed. An NHS manager often cannot meet her or his objectives unless many other value chain participants in, for example, local government and private care facilities also meet theirs. It is highly unlikely that the best of managers (or even GPs) could 'commission' in such a way as to meet all objectives and targets cost-effectively. Clarity and simplification are essential, supported by modern value chain management and relevant capabilities. Too often in health, management is denigrated as a profession. Health management is difficult – if you doubt this, spend some time observing in a hospital – demand and supply rarely balance easily. Integrated, professional management is fundamental to providing successful and cost-effective health and care services. This must include effective and inclusive team management of the many skills and professions involved.

Suggested improvement opportunities

NHS improvements

- Fewer, better defined and planned, more consistent, longer-term initiatives to support agreed objectives.
- Clarity and consistency about what treatments will be provided, nationally and locally, and what will not be. Also, what charges will be levied.
- A renewed focus on outcomes, particularly from the patient's standpoint.
- More emphasis on patient responsibilities for their health.
- Improved information, accounting and governance systems.
- Initiatives to be balanced with managerial capabilities, which must also be improved.
- Managers should not be derided by clinicians. A good doctor or other clinician does not necessarily make a good manager,

but they are fundamental team members. Team management and motivation need to be rediscovered where these are missing.
- Need to improve the integration of physical and mental health services and to link better with local government care services. Need to enhance the links between urgent treatments and ongoing aftercare, in order to deliver better outcomes, eg a major operation should not lead to some permanent disability where several therapies can and should be provided, or at least be strongly recommended.

Value chain management

- Well-designed business processes to support realistic objectives.
- Re-organizations should support objectives and processes and be focused, limited, sustained and well managed.
- Develop integrated objectives and resources appropriate to each locality.
- Realistic assessment of the timescales and costs involved in making major changes, eg closing a large regional care home in order to provide better local care in the community takes a great deal of resources, funding and time.
- Manage related acute physical and mental facilities, clinics, GPs, community care, appropriate to a locality, within an integrated operational and financial structure.
- Improved data architecture to support process architecture.
- Substantially improved project management.
- Use evolutionary prototyping to test and evaluate first on a small scale, before undertaking massive reorganizations or launching complex initiatives and projects.
- Funding and expenditure mechanisms need to be consistent and not produce arbitrary surpluses and deficits.
- Mechanisms are needed to integrate the plans of the various increasingly independent bodies that provide health and care services.
- Need to integrate and professionalize the various procurement and supply activities and not to fragment them.

Strengths

- Many dedicated and skilled workers.
- Huge resources in terms of facilities and funds.
- Enjoys the confidence and goodwill of most people, who want it to continue and do even better.
- No meaningful alternative to the NHS.
- There are a number of very good organizations which should be fostered, eg National Institute for Clinical Excellence (NICE), Royal College of General Practitioners.

Weaknesses

- A political football.
- A plethora of silos.
- Very expensive and inadequate information and computer systems, eg Connecting for Health – with poor project definition and management leading to vast waste of resources.
- Some key resources, especially GPs and some consultants, are paid for by the NHS, but it has limited control over them.
- Attempts to use market forces to improve cost efficiencies rather than to simplify structures and initiatives and to manage these well.
- At the 'mercy' of the international pharmaceutical industry.
- Both funding and expenditure are fragmented over many bodies which have limited incentives to collaborate.
- PCTs, which should control local commissioning, were too weak and often too large – now abolished. Replaced by GP-led Clinical Commissioning Groups (CCGs), which have limited chances of improving such a large and complex value chain, especially since GPs will be substantially motivated by what is in their financial and social self-interest. A new and increasingly complex hierarchy of bureaucrats remains. Leaderships of the NHS and DoH are too often not fit for purpose.

- GPs and other healthcare professionals cannot be guaranteed or even expected to pursue patient benefits at the expense of their own – the last time that GPs had a major vote on pay and conditions of service they decided to take a large pay increase but not provide out-of-hours support (via a nominal reduction in pay). Many senior GP partners now work a four-day week for the NHS and many ordinary non-partner GPs work family-friendly hours. Many doctors and nurses come from abroad – not all have adequate English. Planned changes in pension arrangements are causing some GPs to retire early. Small GP practices are becoming financially precarious because of the growing overheads.
- There is too great a reliance on external management consultancies, notably by the centre.

Proposals

1. Define clearly what will and will not be provided by the state and/or other bodies, at no cost or at defined charges. Develop mechanisms (eg charges) to penalize self-inflicted illnesses, such as drunk people arriving in A&E, and also much of the affliction caused by substance abuse. Redefine what people must do to improve their own health, what the state and NHS will do to assist and what the consequences will be if people are irresponsible in relation to their health.

2. Redefine the value of a human life, eg to the individual, the family, the economy, the community and the nation. What is the net added value of each treatment: benefit versus cost? Is it the extension of a lifespan? Does this depend on the age of a patient – a baby, a student, an employee, a parent, a pensioner? For example, is the future net value of a pensioner's added years (paying income tax now and having paid past tax) worth more or less than that of other groups? Or are we all truly equal?

3. Endeavour to re-focus on the patient and their overall condition and needs. What outcomes does the patient need and how best can these be delivered?

4 Minimize the effects of clinical silos concentrating on the treatments they each provide by nominating one professional to oversee the patient's care while in a particular institution or treatment channel.

5 Develop much better procedures for costing, charging, funding and management accounting.

6 Develop better methods of auditing in order to promote best practice, reduce costs and prevent fraud. The Audit Commission, which was abolished, did a relatively good job for the NHS and for local government. Its abolition has added to the responsibilities of the National Audit Office. The Care Quality Commission (CQC) does much important auditing of premises and activities, but it has a reputation for box ticking and for losing sight of its effect on the patients and users.

7 Redefine which areas require a new integrated approach to health and care, eg the local acute and also mental hospitals, GPs and clinics, care and support facilities, all under a local integrated management team with five-year plans and budgets. London is different from other industrial conurbations, which are different from more and less populated rural areas. One size does not fit all.

8 Develop fresh approaches to the capabilities required for managing the health and care value chain. Recognize that staff need encouraging and motivating as well as managing. Tackle any bullying.

9 Reconsider the training of nurses (and doctors). Establish early on whether an individual is suited to nursing (and dealing directly with people and their medical problems) before entering the nurse on (over-)academic training.

10 Undertake better forecasting, planning and training of each type of key skill.

11 Improve the facilities and resources for recognizing and tackling health problems earlier. This can save major problems and costs later – eg behavioural problems in young children.

Notes

1   Fulford, B, Peile, R and Carroll, H (2012) *Essential Values-Based Practice: Clinical stories linking science with people*, Cambridge University Press, Cambridge
2   Goldacre, B (2014) *I Think You'll Find It's a Bit More Complicated Than That*, Fourth Estate, London

6B.3 Defence equipment (materiel) value chain

Core purpose

To equip and support our armed forces for current and future operations in order to:

- defend the UK and its interests;
- strengthen international peace and stability;
- act as a force for good in the world.

Strategy

Working together with industrial and military partners to:

- Produce battle-winning equipment and equipment support in time. Equipment consists of a platform (eg tank, submarine, aircraft), a major system (eg combat systems, communications and weapon-handling arrangements), plus technical support and related systems.
- Overcome emerging and new threats and instabilities, including cyber threats to systems security.
- Maintain flexible force structures.
- Achieve objectives within authorized funding limits.
- Support the latest Strategic Defence Review, although it is some time since there has been a realistic and thorough review (ie in 1996).

Objectives

- To achieve those set by the government in defence planning assumptions (DPAs), which endeavour to look 20–30 years into the future.
- To meet the 'reasonable' requirements of the government of the day.
- To sustain strategic onshore industrial capacities and capabilities through R&D, design, build and acquisition.
- To provide in-service support and enhancement of military equipment and services.

Plan

- Equipment capability and then procurement/acquisition plans are made 10 years in advance, and should balance the demand for military capability with the potential supply of equipment, systems and platforms. However, there are always emerging longer-term capabilities which need to be incorporated within defence plans.
- Operational plans are usually well done. The joint end-to-end supply chain to forces usually works well, given planning forecasts that fall within the DPAs.
- Four-year financial plans
- Business plans
  - Approved through project-orientated business cases, plus the plans prepared by each operational function and by each of the three Services (Navy, Army, Air Force). These plans define what the Ministry of Defence and its partners (other governments, armed forces and industry) need to do.
  - Note, complex business plans are often less well done than military operational plans.
- Training – all equipment users need substantial, coordinated and ongoing training.

Measures/targets/KPIs/SLAs

- Meeting urgent operational requirements (UORs). These are funded separately by HM Treasury.
- Achieving financial, performance and timing objectives set out in the Equipment Plan for new Capabilities.
- Achieving financial objectives for support to operations within four-year plans.
- Ability of UK forces successfully to conduct real and modelled war scenarios of particular intensities.
- Systems and platforms at required states of readiness.
- Recruit, retain and motivate personnel, especially for project management and technical roles.
- Increase value for money by improving efficiency and effectiveness of key processes, eg reduction of 2.5 per cent per annum of annual expenditure for defined activities.
- Meet short-term budget and cash targets from the government of the day.

It is essential to remember that truly successful defence is *not* having to deploy men and equipment, since their existence is sufficient deterrence.

Analysis and some solutions

Funds are always tight nationally for all public purposes. The Peace Dividend (it was thought that with the demise of the Soviet Union much less resource would be needed to maintain peace and security in Eastern Europe) implied that peace could be maintained at a lower total defence cost. In practice, more military operations have been taking place at a much higher total cost, leaving substantially less money for maintaining force readiness and for developing future capabilities. Furthermore, while conventional warfare capabilities have to be maintained, new types of enemy (terrorists and cyber criminals) require additional capabilities both for defence and for attack. The shortage of funds can result in a hollowing out (delaying expenditure on maintenance and enhancements until they become urgent) of current capabilities because of the great total demand on funds.

1. There is a NATO commitment to spend 2 per cent of GDP on defence, but defining 'defence' can involve conflicting assumptions.

2. Defence customers and end users are a complex combination of: the Chiefs of Staff of the armed forces (often three years in post); government ministers (often changing); the Treasury; Ministry of Defence Permanent (often changing) Secretaries and other top brass; we the people, including taxpayers; allies, including NATO and the United States; our military personnel; our integrated project teams. Defining and achieving consensus is difficult to achieve.

3. New defence equipment capabilities are usually ever more complex, need more integration, software, training and support facilities, and are thereby more expensive. Fewer units are needed and can be afforded. Hence there is less room to learn from experience in defence acquisition. Uncertainties are great, risks are substantial, and there is sometimes inadequate R&D to mitigate these. Therefore a more rigorous approach is required, involving both the evaluation of opportunities and the definition and mitigation of risks, plus better R&D.

4. Preserving and updating nuclear submarines and missiles are very expensive. Can Britain afford these costs? Can Britain maintain adequate deterrence and be a top military power without nuclear facilities?

5. Most equipment is now subject to joint international demand and supply. This adds greatly to uncertainty and risk in agreeing specifications and suppliers, and in managing project results. Therefore, although estimated average cost per unit may be lower, total final cost can be much higher. Consider the provision of two new aircraft carriers, which obviously require appropriate aircraft, which in turn must first meet US (and other nations') requirements for land-based jets. Who knows what the final total cost and delivery dates will be?

6 The Defence Industrial Strategy was intended to develop more effective longer-term collaboration between UK industry and the MoD, with less contractual price competition and lower through-life costs. The jury is still out on how cost-effective these necessary longer-term relationships are. The general shortage of public funds, the continuing annuality of much MoD financing and the difficulty of balancing public procurement competition principles with the development of longer-term collaborative working challenge all existing and developing collaborative relationships with key suppliers. These are not only the major prime contractors, but also certain smaller specialist suppliers. Furthermore, many suppliers are international defence and engineering contractors for whom the UK may not be their main customer. Enhanced MoD management capabilities are essential to manage all the above well.

7 The ability accurately to forecast, plan and implement in relation to performance (capability), contract cost, through-life cost and time factors needs substantial improvement both in the MoD and in industry. Trade-offs need to be more systematic and rigorous. Three-point estimates (see Chapter 11) based on normal distributions are inappropriate and misleading since they imply that the opportunities to improve on estimates are equal to the downside risks, and this is rarely the case. Earned value management should be enhanced and be in more widespread successful operation.

8 The definition and management of uncertainty and risk have been improving; but much remains to be done. Traditionally, civil servants have seen themselves as risk averse rather than risk aware, and this is not helped by the public sector having believed that operational and financial risks can be transferred to suppliers through the contracting process, instead of identifying uncertainties and risks and strongly owning and managing them – when the ammunition is not available or the gun does not fire, who owns the risk? More systematic and rigorous effort needs to be put into defining, and de-risking, such complex projects well at the beginning, beyond scrutinizing and reviewing projects afterwards. Demand and supply must be balanced on an ongoing cost-effective basis at levels of risk which are understood and accepted by the key stakeholders. As a result of my work with defence (and also with health, trade and industry and food), I developed some important solutions to defining and mitigating uncertainty and risks and to structuring and managing complex projects and initiatives. These are detailed in Chapters 11 and 12, and also in my paper 'Improving value and certainty in defence procurement' for the Chartered Institute of Public Finance and Accounting, in *Public Money & Management*, November 2011.

9 Through-life costs can be many times the cost of procurement. The facilities to maintain modern defence capabilities are expensive and complex. Consequently, sound planning and management of the comprehensive overall value chains is an essential part of any defence acquisition programme.

10 The general quality and motivation of staff are often high. However, the capability to design and manage complex projects is inadequate because too many managers (and especially within the military) are not in post sufficiently long to gain and to apply the special capabilities required. Time in post must relate to the job to be done and not to traditional armed forces career progression. Furthermore, the social anthropology of defence is complex – only health has as many tribes and customs, but fewer uniforms. It is not easy nor sometimes wise to balance the membership of project teams across the three Services. As in all value chains, determine the required capabilities and ensure that these are put in place and retained.

11 The science and practice of logistics began with the military (Napoleonic France – *le maréchal des logis* – Quartermaster General). Logistical skills are usually of a high order, although cost-effectiveness could be substantially improved. More comprehensive value chain management skills should be applied, with substantial benefit across customers and suppliers. Business management training is too 'soft'.

12 The ability to track and trace, and therefore to manage items from their sources to the battlefield, has improved substantially. Radio-frequency identification (RFID) tags have been applied to containers within shipments. It is much more difficult to track individual items through to the point of use, partly because of the often very difficult circumstances at or near the front line, and partly because units have traditionally hung onto whatever items they could in case of shortages later.

13 Value chains are sometimes not well understood by the MoD, as contracts can be aggregated to too great a level and placed with large prime contractors. While it can be time-consuming and require particular experience and capability to establish who the critical suppliers are, this is essential, particularly when software or special equipment need to be developed. It is essential to know who are the best-of-breed suppliers for each specialist supply market. Some defence equipment suppliers are not necessarily noted for being highly cost-effective in their private sector work. It is easy to blame the MoD for poor procurement, but it cannot be better than its suppliers. Thus it was very surprising to see the MoD suggest that procurement should become government owned, contractor operated (GOCO). Fortunately, this proposal bit the dust (NOGOCO). However, private sector skills are being imported into the MoD, but it is unclear from which hitherto undiscovered pool of talent – ie what projects in the private sector which have similar complexity to defence projects are likely to provide this available fresh talent?

14 It is too easy for the large suppliers to beat a direct path to government ministers and Chiefs of Staff, bypassing their particular MoD project teams. Control such access.

15 Embedded software is highly complex, and can account for 25 per cent of the cost of defence equipment. The Systems Software Engineering Initiative was established to improve performance in this area. This area needs more investment.

16 Although there are longer-term plans and funding, too great an emphasis is still placed by the Treasury on annual budgets and

cash requirements. Therefore, while there are valuable longer-term capability and military plans, the detailed business plans must become more dependable, looking ahead over several years.

17 As part of the process of improving the understanding of value chains and their management, value chain data and information need to be made more complete and accurate. E-business and IT systems have had variable success but are essential components.

18 Substantial strides have been taken to improve collaborative electronic design and development of new equipment, with the support of the UK Council for Electronic Business.

19 Contracting mechanisms need further enhancement to help define, promote and reward mutually beneficial performance by industry.

6B.4 Passenger transport – rail, road, air, sea

Core purpose

- To deliver people on time to where they want to be at prices they are willing to pay.
- To promote economic and social development through linking homes to workplaces, shops and recreational activities.
- To attract overseas visitors.
- To sustain rural communities.
- To reduce congestion and pollution by private vehicles.

Strategy

Defines in appropriate detail:

- types of service and coverage;
- publicly vs privately owned transport; general vs individual transport; private car usage; movement of freight as well as people;

- provision of parking;
- role of competition;
- total expenditure including subsidies, and payments by operators to government agencies;
- types of charge to end users;
- types of subsidy, by service, by citizen group;
- R&D on current and potential forms of transport;
- environmental standards;
- development of corporate reputations and brand values;
- resilience planning, eg energy and fuel availability; labour availability; coping with extreme weather;
- effective security measures – in relation to means of transport and in relation to types of passenger, eg overseas travel, Channel Tunnel;
- maintenance and enhancements of equipment and facilities.

Objectives

- Service levels – where, on time, in comfort (lack of over-crowding).
- Passenger safety and security.
- Effective and integrated timetables.
- Defined, reasonable prices producing agreed levels of revenue.
- Sustainable profit levels for the service providers.
- Public cost/subsidy levels which are cost-effective for the public authorities responsible for transport.
- Stimulating economic growth and productivity through good, cost-effective service for people and freight, and through major investments. HS2 and York–Leeds–Manchester–Liverpool rail links have been proposed in order to meet these objectives. However, it is not difficult to question the calculations justifying these projects. What will the total costs finally be? When will they be up and running? What will be the net

benefit to the regions? How many major railway stations can Birmingham railway users sensibly employ (New Street, International and a new HS2 terminal)? What economic and social benefits will actually be realized and when? What investment alternatives are there with earlier and better benefit/cost ratios and fewer risks? These examples indicate how important it is to develop an agreed, rigorous methodology for justifying investments.

- Load factors and improvements in transport productivity.
- Customer satisfaction.
- Repeat business.
- Market shares as they affect the sustainability of a service or its value for money to the user.
- Satisfying regulators and public bodies.
- Encouraging airlines, railway companies, bus companies, taxi companies, ferry operators through adequate levels of revenue and profit.
- Developing pricing structures reflecting competitive factors and monopolistic elements – relating to routes, timetables and facilities.
- Helping older people travel more through bus and rail passes. The value of a bus pass relates not only to who uses it but also to the viability of the service for all.

How consistent and realistic are all these? These need fresh examination from the point of view of the users, each transport company and of the Department of Transport, local government and regulators.

Plan

- Passenger volumes per type of transport and area.
- Timetables indicating what integrated services it is intended to provide. Timetables are plans and need to be reliable.
- Capital investment on transport and infrastructure and associated annual and through- life revenue expenditures.

- Prices, income, margins.
- Licence charges.
- Government charges, taxation.
- R&D.
- Training.
- Weather/resilience contingency plan.
- See also Chapter 10 on planning.
- There has been a lack of sustained and integrated transport planning over many years.

Measures/targets/KPIs

- Costs and fares per passenger mile for each type of transport – effects on the cost of living.
- Comparisons with private car costs.
- Comparisons with other countries.
- Timeliness.
- Accidents per passenger mile.
- Environmental costs and charges.
- Subsidies to and payments by transport companies to the government.
- Ridership.
- Patronage.
- Passenger numbers.
- Fare receipts.
- Complaints.

Issues

The first issue is that the passenger transport value chain is greatly affected by other value chains – freight transport; housing; industry; and many others. Competition within and between, and integration of, transport types and related value chains have not been well directed over many years – nationally, regionally and often locally.

As an example of this, please consider in relation to where you live and work how satisfied you are with: the availability and cost of each type of public transport; the timeliness and comfort of services; the effects on road congestion and road safety; the availability and cost of parking; the availability of Park and Ride schemes; the availability of taxis and their charges; the role of cycling; pedestrians and pedestrianization; the effects on the quality of air and other environmental factors; the investment plans for your area in relation to housing, business and industrial development and the consequential effects on transport needs; the capabilities of those individuals and organizations reportedly responsible for transport planning and management; the management of change; communications with transport operators and authorities; integration with public utility roadworks.

Transportation investment needs to be related to other plans such as housing, industry and leisure. It is disappointing how often major developments are proposed for an area without public and private transport considerations being thought-through; for example, York Council leaders often propose expansion plans for housing and industry in order to improve the financial situation, but have limited ideas on how to cope with existing major traffic problems, let alone with the inevitable consequences of expansion.

Other issues to consider include:

- Relationships with urban railways, underground systems and trams need careful consideration.

- There is an unclear relationship between transport subsidies and taxes and costs.

- The structures and attitudes of regulatory bodies keep changing, eg rail. The West Coast Rail Franchise calculations were badly done by the Department of Transport and its advisers, and the franchising had to be redone. The new tramways in Croydon/Wimbledon are seen by some to be successful, while the Edinburgh tram system has been very expensive, late and incomplete. However, I leave you to think about your own environs.

- Balancing national economic benefits of freight versus passenger traffic is an ongoing process.
- Balancing national economic needs versus environmental targets and local pressures is always very difficult, eg airport expansion.
- Congestion charging and traffic bans are being considered and implemented here and there across the UK. Some people argue that the expansion of the Uber app would allow many more cars to be hired by the public at a lower cost than the normal licensed taxis. Others argue that this would add many more vehicles to already overcrowded roads. Why not undertake some rigorous value chain analysis?
- Pollution continues to grow in all major cities.
- Rural communities depend for their survival on transport availability at reasonable charges.
- Older people use their bus passes not only to shop and to visit friends but also to remain active in the community. Removing or limiting this benefit might also make overall bus services less viable.

Considering all the above, there is great merit in a thorough review of the overall transport value chains. It is time to employ some rigorous value chain analysis and arithmetic. This review would include public transport in relation to freshly agreed objectives, including national and local economic, social, energy, environmental and security factors. This review should also produce more integrated and effective legislation and governance.

6B.5 The water value chain: structure and added value

Core purpose

The water and sewerage industry in England and Wales provides end-to-end water supply, wastewater treatment and discharge services to both households and businesses. Clean water is essential to life. It needs to be provided in a useable form to homes, businesses and all locations where people live and work. It needs to be removed from where it is not wanted and made safe when polluted.

Strategy and practice

Within the UK the water and sewage industry can be characterized as a natural monopoly, since historically, and for economic, social and environmental reasons, only one supplier exists to the end consumers. Consumers may have some choice about the services they receive (eg private boreholes or waste treatment), but this is very limited. The structure of the industry has been inherited from pre-privatization public sector companies, generally based on geographic catchment areas. The companies were privatized in 1989 and made subject to separate economic and quality regulation, now undertaken by the Water Services Regulation Authority (Ofwat).

The industry serves 31 million properties through 340,000 km of water mains and 550,000 km of sewers. It directly employs 38,000 with an estimated additional 100,000 people through the directly related supply chain. Annual turnover is £11.5bn on assets with a net worth of £46bn.

In theory the value chain is straightforward. Water companies own rights to extract water from rivers and lakes, and to store it in surface and groundwater reservoirs – they own about 90 per cent of these regulatory licences. Raw water itself is not ascribed an economic value – this arises from the activities to treat and distribute the product to the end customer. Charges to the end customer may be based on metered water usage, or charged on a historic local council 'rateable value' property basis.

Wastewater (sewerage) treatment includes a number of additional products – foul sewage removal from properties, surface water drainage (from buildings and impermeable areas such as car parks) and highway drainage. Drains and sewers flow to sewage treatment works, with water returned to the environment, and sludge treated and supplied to farmers as a fertilizer or used to generate electricity. Except for higher-strength 'trade effluent' from businesses that need a specific licence, the service supplied is not directly measured. For most customers, charges for sewerage services are based on the water volume, with a standard allowance for water not returned as foul.

Objectives

The reliable provision of clean water to where people need it is a key objective which is legally enforced. The relationship with the customer has, historically, been based on a legal duty to supply rather than based on contracts, in particular for 'domestic' use – liability to pay rests with the occupier rather than the owner of a property. There is also no legal ability for suppliers to disconnect households for non-payment. In many situations, suppliers can include commercial enterprises that 'resell' water and sewerage services to domestic consumers (eg sheltered housing companies).

Suppliers are required to provide infrastructure to support housing development. There is a market for providing infrastructure on development sites. The water and sewerage companies may pay developers to adopt sites rather than being required themselves to undertake the on-site work; that is water suppliers can agree that developers will undertake some on-site work for which they will receive certain rebates. For new developments, an alternative supplier can become the monopoly service provider to the new properties, receiving a bulk supply of water and wastewater services from the regional supplier. Developers have a right to connect into the public sewerage network. A 'tax' in the form of an infrastructure charge per property helps to fund the wider network for new developments.

Resource constraints for water supply reflect the fact that variability in weather conditions can have the potential to impact both the supply of water resources and the demand of customers (for instance, peak usage in hot dry weather). With low elasticity of demand with respect to price (circa –0.1 has been estimated; ie even if the price doubled, demand would only decline by 10 per cent), and with regulation restricting the potential to adjust prices in any case, non-price incentives for customers voluntarily to reduce demand (ie encouraging water efficiency) are important.

Ultimately, customers do have limited ability to substitute other forms of delivery for public water. For instance, even the cheapest bottled water is c. 500 times more expensive than tap water. Customers are not in a position to make choices about the quality of water that is supplied, and this is therefore heavily regulated. There are options available to customers in terms of the quality and reliability of the water supplied. For instance, customers in hard-water areas on average spend £80 per annum more on water softening and water filters than in soft-water areas, which generally outweighs the higher cost of public water supply for soft water. Taste preferences of consumers are often framed by what they are used to, with even minor changes being noticed between regions or when companies change supply sources during droughts.

A number of related products are often provided outside of the standard water and sewerage services within a competitive market, but remain a relatively small part of the value chain. These include treatment of tankered waste, laboratory services, property search information and a number of other supply-related services.

Measures

Dependability of supply. Consistent quality/taste of water. Meeting EU directives for standards. Total costs of providing water and sewerage. Prevention of flooding. Levels of investment. Returns to shareholders. Disruptions to everyday life from work on pipes and sewers (especially when other utilities are also working in the same area).

Analysis and proposals

Aspects of supply

Although the water and sewerage suppliers are regional monopolies, there is a wider variety of operating models and methods of interacting with the value chain. The supply side is diverse, ranging from large multinational construction, engineering and consultancy firms to local specialist suppliers. Procurement models are therefore similarly diverse. Many activities can be provided on an in-sourced or outsourced basis (ranging from operations, construction, design, meter reading, call centres and billing). Alliance partnership models with a mixture of directly employed and supplier staff working together under one management and commercial framework are also used.

There is a large equipment, service and consultancy supply chain, which ranges from specialist local firms to global multinationals. The UK has a strategic advantage with a historic background in water and wastewater treatment research and has a strong export platform in water engineering products and consultancy. The commercial and economic regulation framework is more developed than in most other countries, and this is exported as a model where private finance is needed to support investment to be funded over time by customers and where public sector financing is constrained.

For what is fundamentally an essential public service, the question as to why the industry is better established through a value chain driven by market forces rather than government control and ownership is always topical. In Scotland the water industry remains public owned and financed, but with retail competition for business customers, with new private sector entrants competing with the public incumbent. A private/shareholder ownership model helps to attract necessary long-term investment, but the degree to which this model represents customers' interests will always be open to challenge, particularly where foreign ownership and complex financing/tax structures are involved. Ultimately, regulation of the industry, irrespective of the ownership structure, has to protect a diverse range of customer interests.

Regulation and incentives

With the industry largely considered a natural monopoly, price regulation is used to protect consumers. This has traditionally focused on comparative competition – comparing the cost efficiency and service levels of the different regional monopolies and then setting future prices to reflect future investment and service needs, net of efficiency targets. Companies could outperform (through delivering productive efficiencies) and enhance shareholder value by delivering specific outputs at a lower cost than targeted. The scope of these gains (and in particular the rewards for innovating for new services and for dynamic efficiency through working in ways that add more value) is small compared to the potential for financing and tax allowance outperformance, relative to the cost of capital assumed by the economic regulator (Ofwat) when setting prices.

Returns on investment are protected by licences, which provide a degree of trust for investors that past investment will continue to receive an adequate return. Appeal mechanisms are also in place should the regulator set returns lower than justified by market evidence, or with insufficient cost allowances for future requirements.

However, a number of regulatory and government policy changes are challenging the status quo of the value chain for the industry:

- Transition of the regulatory framework incentivizing the delivery of fixed outputs to a focus on outcomes. An example of an output would be monitoring that a specific property had been protected from flooding with a physical asset change. An outcome alternative would monitor and incentivize how many customer properties are flooded
- All business customers having a choice of retailer (meter reading, account management and billing services) from 1 April 2017 – with the likely impact ultimately being de-regulation of pricing for this element of the value chain. The potential for existing companies to exit this part of the market was included within the Water Act 2014.
- Upstream competition for wholesale activities after 2019, in particular water resources and sludge treatment and disposal.
- Greater potential for mergers between regional companies and for firms to specialize in specific parts of the value chain.

Investors

Financing of investment is a significant part of the value chain. In the past 25 years the industry has been required to improve significantly both drinking water and wastewater quality in order to allow the UK to meet the requirements of EU directives. Increased investment is likely to continue for the foreseeable future in order to meet new quality standards and customer/environmental policy requirements for both water and wastewater. New investment is not cash funded up front in the regulatory regime, with a regulatory capital value (RCV) built up on which a rate of return is earned. The RCV is index linked to the Retail Price Index, which since 2010 has resulted in a very low cost of financing being possible for the industry; for example, 2.6 per cent real return is assumed by Ofwat in setting prices for 2015.

Markets

The consideration of whether more market forces can be used within the industry does not mean that a core element of the provision of water and sewerage services will cease to be a natural monopoly – in particular, it is highly unlikely to be economic for competing pipework to be laid by other suppliers in order to distribute water and sewerage. Unlike electricity and gas, a national grid does not exist, and again this is limited by physical geography and the large amount of energy required to distribute product. The lack of a water grid can mean that one part of the country can experience drought conditions while another area has full reservoirs.

Another distinction from energy markets is that there is no wholesale market for water resources or sludge – property rights exist for abstracting water from the environment through regulatory licences, without an effective and simple trading market existing (trades have to be agreed with regulators who set terms and conditions). There are a number of environmental barriers to overcome for a resource market to exist – notably the local conditions placed on abstraction licences, and the environmental impact of an abstraction that varies depending on the use to which the water is put and how much of this used water ultimately returns to the environment. For instance, storing water in reservoirs that can be released when river flow is low (not just for public water supply purposes) has environmental benefits, but there is no specific economic value from this activity – it is governed by abstraction licence conditions instead.

Similarly, pipework is not the only element of likely natural monopoly. In many circumstances, water and wastewater treatment works have to be considered along with the network when assessing capacity constraints for supporting development sites, even though in theory innovation in treatment processes could arise from a competitive market for this activity.

However, given the nature of the water value chain, there may be more benefit in developing markets for complementary activities, rather than just focusing on where competition could replace the economic regulation of regional monopolies:

- Paid ecosystem services – markets that provide incentives for landowners to improve water quality and reduce environmental problems in the long term. In future this will avoid water companies/water customers funding 'end of pipe' treatment improvements in the supply chain (innovation) – such as competition for the market in providing new infrastructure for developers and new treatment facilities.

- Business retail market – specialist services to support the new market, such as brokers and water efficiency experts.
- Wholesalers to retailer services – for example, it may be more efficient for retailers to outsource activities they are responsible for, such as meter reading, to those that own the meter asset (wholesalers).
- Upstream markets – for instance, alternative routes for disposing of sewage sludge (feedstock for incinerators rather than a free fertilizer to agriculture).
- Potential for more integrated solutions to urban flooding – planning urban development and flood prevention on a wider basis (eg maintenance of green spaces that store surface water in wet periods rather than overloading the sewerage system).
- Energy generation – water resources and sludge are already used for energy generation, but market developments could optimize their use further.

Customer perspective

Ultimately, the value generation potential of the water and wastewater value chain should be seen from a long-term customer/consumer perspective. Investment that is made now commits customers to pay for this level of service over the life of the asset, which can be more than 100 years.

The retail market for business customers only represents about 5 per cent of the cost to serve, with approximately 50 per cent of this representing a potential profit margin from which a retailer has to fund acquisition cost, market risk and working capital. However, this underestimates the potential value to customers from developing the market. Bigger gains are likely to result from: reduced admin costs arising from water and retail services (better customer services/fewer bills); consolidated information on multiple sites through electronic data interchange and e-business – see Chapters 7 and 8; and bespoke and tailored specialist advice and services that encourage reduced water consumption, which current suppliers do not have an incentive to provide as part of the mass service provision to customers as a whole.

Government policy currently restricts the retail market to businesses, on the grounds that any alternative gains are unlikely to be significant enough for household customers. For them, social protection (including social tariff cross-subsidies between customers) outweighs the potential market benefits.

Challenges to value chain decisions

Upstream markets face barriers, in particular identifying the value chain for an individual market area without losing the benefits of integration across the whole. This particularly applies because many of the benefits of a planned policy rather than a market approach potentially only apply in the long term. The decision on a policy vs market approach to future planning therefore depends on the degree to which future risk and uncertainty can be considered in any market or non-market decision-making approach.

The key factors to be taken into account are: a long asset life and sunk cost of committing to some decisions now; and externalities – considering social and environmental public as well as private consequences.

Regulated business investment decisions (and the outcome incentives used to protect customer interest and to provide a risk and reward framework for investors in the value chain) are assessed in order to take into account: (a) the future private cost risk to the company if investment is not made (eg higher costs of treatment if asset performance reduces); and (b) the social and environmental consequences in the future of inaction (eg customer willingness to pay to avoid increased flooding). This reflects the wider policy objectives that the government sets for the sector. However, a successful upstream market needs to retain the inclusion of future risks in the incentives and market framework.

This is a challenging prospect – many of the external factors affecting the industry arise from social and sustainability trends that are inherently unpredictable. It is challenging for any individual company's decision-making process to take account of these factors, particularly where there is an absence of data or knowledge ('unknown unknown' risks and opportunities). Defining market mechanisms that can adapt as new data knowledge emerges while maintaining infrastructure investment is the key challenge for the water value chain. The decision on whether to use a market framework or retain a monopoly approach requires widespread engagement and transparency on the objectives. Only then can the key barriers to realizing value in a market framework be overcome (in particular, how to price individual value chain activities given the huge diversity of the local value chains for water and wastewater services between regions).

Water and the environment

Everyone needs clean water and fresh air and acceptable temperatures within reasonably predictable climates. Should there be integrated value chain management to meet these objectives? The Meteorological Office tries to predict weather, but not its consequences. The water industry captures the water it needs, routes it to where it is needed, and also disposes of sewage. The Environment Agency (within the Department for Food, Agriculture and Rural Affairs) endeavours to cope with water in the wrong places with an emphasis on farmland and the countryside. Local authorities oversee the places where people live and work, including the effects of flooding and air pollution. The Department for Transport concerns itself with transport and pays some attention to air pollution. The Department for Energy and Climate Change tries to encourage cost-effective and secure supplies of energy at the same time as considering how energy provision might mitigate climate change. Clearly there needs to be fresh consideration of what integrated and cost-effective objectives should be set and how these should be realized. What integrated value chains should be developed to serve us?

A review of some modern value chains

6C

REFORM OF KEY INSTITUTIONS

6C.1 Reform of the government value chain

Core purpose

A government exists to direct a country, society, the economy and the public, private and voluntary sectors. A government should decide clearly what activities it will undertake itself, what it will leave to the various markets, what it will leave to individual citizens and to the voluntary sector, and how all these should be regulated, or not. All other value chains are fundamentally affected by the government value chain.

A government's core purpose should be defined in its election manifesto and elaborated in White Papers and other policy documents. Too often these lack precision. We should distinguish between the core purpose of government and the core purpose of a particular government. The same applies to objectives and plans – compare what is offered with what you think is required and define what is missing.

Ideally a government should be democratically elected by a majority of the electorate, and it should be accountable on an agreed, regular basis to the electorate. A government should comprise:

1 A primary parliamentary chamber (such as the House of Commons, or Chamber of Deputies), elected by the people to

agree to legislation and to oversee all that affects the state and the citizens. A fundamental role of the Members of Parliament is to represent their constituents both collectively and also individually when practicable, in order to help them achieve their objectives and to overcome their problems.

2 Ministers overseeing government departments, and responsible to the primary chamber. There should be a prime minister, premier or first minister to lead the government.

3 Civil servants developing policies and drafting legislation and managing the government departments and agencies. Reporting to the ministers.

4 A second chamber to review and enhance the decisions of the primary chamber.

5 A head of state, who may be elected or hereditary.

6 Corresponding levels of local government.

A government should focus on improving and securing the well-being of the people in relation to health and care, standard of living, education, creativity, employment, housing, energy and other key public utilities, finance, transport, environment, safety and security, justice and rule of law, communications and their media.

Strategy

Candidates for election to Parliament, and their various political parties, publish a manifesto stating what they intend to achieve. These manifestos and subsequent White Papers and policy documents vary greatly in detail and in practicality. They can be thwarted by reality, by events, by external forces, by lack of resources and by incompetence.

How can we improve the performance of our governments and our democracy? How can we optimize the value added by our government?

Many actions by our government are substantially affected by other governments and international organizations. What changes are required to the following value chains – the European Union, the United States, United Nations, NATO, Russia, China, Middle East…?

What decisions should be the responsibility of government and what decisions should be taken by individuals or by market forces?

Democratic values and objectives

1. What principles and values do we wish to adhere to as a democratic nation? Should these values be: equality/equity under the law; equality of opportunity to fulfil individual and group potentials; probity; integrity; ethicality; respect; freedom of speech and belief; effective media? How do we ensure that these principles are meaningfully applied? What values are we thereby trying to realize for society? How do we measure these?

2. What objectives should we set as a nation in order to put these principles into practice and to realize these values? How do we ensure adherence?

3. What value chains will most effectively help us to realize these objectives reliably and cost-effectively?

4. What councils and parliaments should there be, and where? How many seats (per elector, per square mile, per region, per category of voter)? What should be the structure of the second chamber, and on what democratic basis should its members be elected or appointed? What should be the roles, responsibilities, accountabilities, terms of office and procedures for each elected body? What should be the qualifications to vote? What decisions should be left to elected bodies and what decisions should be taken in referendums? What decisions should be taken locally or centrally? Should our system of government become federal, including how little or how much power should rest in the capital city? Power without responsibility is dangerous, and responsibility without power and adequate funding leads inevitably to failure and also to the blame game.

5. What should be the role of a head of state in a democracy? How far above and beyond the ongoing political processes should the head of state stand? What are the benefits of the head of state being above and beyond politics?

6   What do we mean by freedom of speech and of belief? Are there limits to these which a democratic society should have in place? How multi-cultural should a society become, or should it define in detail what it means to be a citizen and facilitate all inhabitants meeting that model?

7   How much say should citizens have in deciding who should stand in an election? Should political parties decide on candidates with no prior reference to the electorate – or should there be open primary elections (see below in 'Reforming our democratic value chain'), at which any citizen can stand for election, with a primary focus on the capabilities that each candidate brings to the particular office and role? Can we have an effective democracy if the electorate are simply choosing between political parties? After all, what say do all the citizens have in how a political party is run?

8   How should political parties be controlled by the citizens? What limits should be placed on political party democracy, governance, funding and behaviours? Given our nation's objectives, what capabilities are required for an individual to be a successful councillor, Member of Parliament, government minister or senior civil servant? What collective capabilities are needed within each government body – variety, balance, compatibility? How should these capabilities be determined, published and applied? Answering these questions well depends on what is each body's role. What government departments or agencies do we need to undertake well-specified objectives, and how should each be structured? Thereby, what should each government minister be responsible for? What should each civil servant be answerable for? Why, for example, does it make economic and strategic (rather than political) sense to link Energy and Climate Change, or Culture, Media and Sport?

9   How should governmental initiatives be defined, justified, agreed and implemented – including benefits/outcomes/added value, costs (capital, running, through-life), opportunities and risks, timescales, management, governance, measurement of

outcomes? What structured arithmetic should be always applied to all key initiatives and projects? Measures of success include GDP per head, state deficits or surpluses, incomes per head of key groups, balance of payments and trade, productivity of all key sectors, levels of employment and unemployment, levels of crime and re-offending, educational attainments, houses built, performance of the National Health Service, numbers of tourists, numbers of immigrants, and so on.

10 What activities should be left to the market? What limitations should be placed on markets and on private companies? For each free market, what basic regulations should be in place to ensure safety and consistency? How should these be enforced? What rights should shareholders have in relation to end users/consumers, employees, managers, directors, governments? Should shareholders be classified according to 'genuine' interest in a business, eg hedge funds vs pension funds, and individuals vs short sellers borrowing shares? How independent should non-executive directors be, and how many should be focused on good governance?

11 In addition to private sector governance, what controls and oversight are needed for the public sector? How do we ensure that Parliament and its Select Committees and also the National Audit Office are wise before the event? That is, problems are anticipated and wise recommendations are made and implemented in time.

12 What goods and services should the state provide for its citizens, for all or for some, for the more or less 'needy' or 'deserving', means-tested or not, provided directly or indirectly, free or at a charge? How should we measure the value of these goods and services – to the individual, to society? How fundamental is it to a genuine democracy to emphasize inclusivity rather than exclusivity?

   a Rule of Law – just and sound law; affordable for all and not just for the few; accountable policing; efficient courts of law; punishment and prison; retribution; rehabilitation. Given that a large proportion of people in prison are mentally ill, to what extent did they 'choose' to break the law, and how best can they be rehabilitated? What should be the limitations on both the legislatures and the judiciary? Why should an individual not be able to defend him or herself well without the costly support of lawyers/barristers? Should all key judging panels, including the Supreme Court, include lay members? Why leave the administration of justice to lawyers? What should be the roles of independent arbitrators?

b Defence and security – anticipated sources of attack on us, on allies, on 'deserving' peoples. What procedures must be followed before we attack people our government does not like? What are the new risks to our defence, such as cyber attacks, terrorism, germ warfare? What constitutes a thorough Strategic Defence Review?

c Education and training – primary, intermediary, tertiary, ongoing – intellectual, vocational. How many UK and overseas students should we educate? What constitutes a balanced education that meets the ongoing and future needs of society? Fundamentally, what aspects of education should be directed and paid for by the state for the longer-term benefit of all?

d Health and care – illnesses and incapacities (physical and mental) – for the young, old, unfit, incapable, careless. How should we define what care should be provided and by whom? 'Care' means not only the desire to care but having the ongoing means of care. To whom do we give individual responsibility for overseeing the treatment and care of each patient, especially those with multiple/complex illnesses and requiring treatment beyond a single institution?

e Finance – sources and uses of funding; rates of interest; terms and conditions. Should commercial banking be entirely separated from investment banking? To what extent should banking be local rather than national or international? How do we ensure effective governance of the financial sector? How do we define what longer-term investments will truly benefit the country and the world? We try to measure gross domestic product, but we have no truly effective measures of the value of the national assets which would bring most benefit to all from further investment, eg a laboratory, hospital, factory, power station, nature reserve, school, road, railway, airport, museum. Would we be better off if the Bank of England, the Treasury and other key economics institutions were staffed with fewer monetarists, who have an excessive preoccupation with interest rates and the supply of money, rather than with sound investments to grow the whole economy. They become very unhappy with very low interest rates and falling prices/deflation. They tend to assume that influencing money supply well will result in the optimal supply of the real goods and services we need.

f Housing – to buy, to rent – affordable or subsidized – location. Do we all 'deserve' decent housing – where, when and at what price? Thereby, how are the appropriate numbers of each type of rented or owned house to be provided?

g Income supplements and benefits, eg unemployment, poverty, incapacity. How should we define minimum standards of living? Who needs or deserves what, when and for how long? How effective are particular threats or promises in motivating people to try harder?

h Energy and other key utilities such as water, communications, mail. Who can we trust to own these and invest in their sound development?

i Transport – road, rail, air, sea – urban/rural.

j Culture for all.

k Sport and fitness.

l Environment – land, air and sea – what standards and where? When?

13 How should these public goods and services be paid for – personal taxation, sales/expenditure taxation, charges, business taxation, local taxes?

14 Does it matter whether or not these are provided directly by the state or via the private sector, or by 'agencies' of the state? For example, could defence be provided by mercenaries, or child protection by profit-making organizations? Does it matter whether or not these are provided by foreign-owned organizations, eg energy supplies, pharmaceutical and other key research areas? Do we believe in the maintenance of vital long-term knowledge and capability in our country (achieved via both researching and implementation, eg nuclear power) for key areas? If it is agreed that private companies are to be used, how should these be policed – how effective do regulators need to be, and how achievable is this?

15 To the extent that some people believe that nationalized industries were inefficient and costly, while others believe that the key private sector suppliers of public services (eg Serco. G4S, Capita, Atos) are inefficient and costly, what is the efficient and cost-effective way forward? We need to learn how to manage more cost-effectively. Should we develop new agencies to undertake certain key state roles?

16 How can the public sector become good/professional at commissioning and procurement? Choosing unwisely between poor suppliers under the disguise of fostering competition is not going to improve matters.

17 Does inequality of income, wealth and power matter? How much inequality damages democracy and society? How much does it matter where and how wealth was accumulated by investors or residents, eg by foreign or British oligarchs or criminals? How much does it matter how people spend their wealth – on private or on public art, on parties or on paupers, on political benefit or for charitable purposes? One could argue that despots over the centuries fostered better art and architecture (? for the few) than modern committees.

18 What should be the roles of communication media – freedom of the press? What constraints are necessary? What controls should there be over media ownership? How much should we pay to preserve and develop the BBC or other public communication bodies?

19 What activities and roles should people perform for and by themselves? What should be the roles of the voluntary sector and what should its relationship be to government? What can we learn from the great success and cost-effectiveness of such bodies as the Royal National Lifeboat Institution and the Hospice Movement?

Further reading: reform of the Government value chain

1 King, A and Crewe, I (2013) *The Blunders of our Governments*, Oneworld, London. Anthony King and Ivor Crewe argue that blunders are not mere mistakes – they are serious and costly errors which could and should have been avoided or greatly mitigated. They are becoming worse. Governments of all parties appear equally blunder-prone – a fact that in itself suggests that there are systemic defects in the British system of government, defects rooted in the culture and institutions of Whitehall and Westminster having little to do with party leaders, party members or partisan ideologies. Our political system specializes in being wise after the event. King and Crewe say that the National Audit Office, the House of Commons Public Accounts Committee and some similar bodies, though not all, are admirable; but they suffer from two limitations – they largely focus on the 'What' questions and they tend to neglect the 'Why' questions – they seldom delve deeply into the causes of whatever went wrong. They seldom explore the decision-making by ministers and officials that led to the committing of the blunder in question. These bodies only rarely step back and try to discern patterns of behaviour.

2 *Dod's Parliamentary Companion* and *Dod's Civil Service Companion*, London – regularly updated. They provide basic data on parliamentarians and civil servants. Too many in government come from the same narrow (and non-quantitative) backgrounds. This is supported by various reviews of the backgrounds of Parliamentarians by the Sutton Trust, Smith Institute etc.

3 So far I have not found any rigorous analysis of the individual and collective capabilities needed for effective government in comparison with what exists.

4 McGuffog, T et al. (2009) *Value Chain Management: Developing a more valuable and certain future*, CILT (in conjunction with CIPS & GS1), London. 'A value chain is the overall set of internal and external resources – human, physical, financial and informational – that require

to be marshalled and managed in order to achieve the objectives of any organization. The management focus is on optimizing net added value for the end user, and for all the key participants in the chain, through defining and managing the entire value chain from beginning to end, by enhancing performance, speed, certainty, safety and security at a low total cost, and at understood and accepted levels of risk.' Various public and private value chains are analysed.

5 McGuffog, T (2011) Improving value and certainty in defence procurement, *Journal of Public Money & Management*, November (also covers improvements to public sector performance).

6 Smith, A (1776) *An Inquiry into the Nature and Causes of the Wealth of Nations*, The Glasgow Edition (1976), Oxford University Press. Adam Smith wrote extensively on competition and its control; on market development and productivity; on trade; on realism in relation to what governments should attempt to achieve; on self-interest; etc.

7 Sandell, M (2013) *What Money Can't Buy: The moral limits of markets*, Penguin, Harmondsworth. Michael Sandell was the 2009 BBC Reith Lecturer. How can we protect the moral and civic goods that markets do not honour and money cannot buy?

8 Owen, D (2008) *In Sickness and In Power*, Methuen, London. David Owen describes the physical and mental illnesses of many world leaders. Many political and other leaders suffer from hubris, which too often leads to nemesis. I suggested to him that one conclusion to draw from his analysis is that there should be a regular, structured assessment test for all government ministers.

9 Goldacre, B (2014) *I Think You'll Find It's a Bit More Complicated Than That*, Fourth Estate, London. Ben Goldacre includes an excellent analysis of the unwise, ill-considered and expensive reforms of the NHS implemented by David Cameron and Andrew Lansley (see pages 169–177).

10 *The Deserted Village* (Oliver Goldsmith's poem of 1770). Could now be The Deserted Factory, The Deserted High Street, The Deserted Housing Development:

> Ill fares the land, to hastening ills a prey,
> Where wealth accumulates and men decay:
> Princes and lords may flourish or may fade;
> A breath can make them as a breath has made;
> But a bold peasantry [*citizenry*], their country's pride,
> When once destroyed can never be supplied.
>
> ———
>
> Ye friends to truth, ye statesmen, who survey
> The rich man's joys increase, the poor's decay,
> 'Tis yours to judge how wide the limits stand
> Between a splendid and an happy land.

> Proud swells the tide with loads of freighted ore [*and oil*],
> And shouting Folly hails them from her shore;
> Hoards, even beyond the miser's wish abound,
> And rich men flock from all the world around.
> Yet count our gains. This wealth is but a name
> That leaves our useful products still the same.
> Not so the loss.

(My updates in italics.) See also Judt, T (2010) *Ill Fares the Land*, Penguin.

11 The Cabinet Office (2013, 18 April) Capabilities Plan, The Cabinet Office, London. This plan appears to be assuming that the necessary capabilities exist within the Civil Service ('a wealth of talent'). It argues that what is required are 'training opportunities' (five days per annum) and 'performance management' to support civil servants to develop the skills and abilities in such areas as 'Commercial Skills' (mainly procurement which government after government has failed to develop well – why do private companies so often find it relatively easy to negotiate contracts which favour them rather than the public sector?), 'Delivering Successful Projects and Programmes' (little evidence to date), 'Redesigning Services and Delivering them Digitally' (a poor track record), and 'Leading and Managing Change' (both politicians and civil servants often tend to select changes unwisely and manage them badly). These recommendations are necessary, but not sufficient, for sustained progress.

12 Bouchal, P and McCrae, J (April 2013) *Financial Leadership for Government*, Institute for Government, London.

13 Lambert, R (2013) Degrees of Debt – the student loans scheme is unsustainable, *Prospect*, May. The new students' loans scheme is a 'perfect' example of incapable government, and also of the inability to calculate likely costs and benefits including risk scenarios. The Treasury needed to cut the National Debt. Therefore, instead of the Treasury funding the universities, students should pay greater fees to the universities by borrowing from the Treasury. Repayments only have to be made if graduate incomes are above £21,000 plus inflation, and are written off after 30 years if unpaid. The universities, being somewhat brighter than the coalition government, have most often set annual fees at the maximum £9,000 in order to enhance the funds paid to them by the Exchequer, and also thereby transferring the risk to it. Instead of reducing government debt by £3bn pa, the scheme could eventually increase it by over £100bn in total. Furthermore, it is likely substantially to inhibit the ability of graduates to save and spend on such items as houses, families and pensions. Underlying this issue is the matter of who benefits from a university education (the individual, society and the economy) and thereby what the priorities should be for teaching and research.

14 'Reform' Think Tank (July 2013) Complete Modernization of our Public Services, 'Reform' Think Tank, London (largely financed by business, and close to the then coalition government). What public services are really needed and how best/low cost can they be delivered – by private or public bodies? 'Reform' says that taxes cannot be increased and should be cut.

15 Major Projects Leadership Academy – founded Feb 2012. Being developed with Deloittes and the Said Business School at Oxford. Too early to tell.

16 Seddon, J (2008) *Systems Thinking in the Public Sector*, Triarchy Press, Axminster. John Seddon describes how bureaucracy and red tape (targets, incentives, inspection) have driven public services in the wrong direction – how to do much better by putting individuals first and replacing blame with genuine responsibility. Also by John Seddon (2014) *The Whitehall Effect*, Triarchy Press, Axminster.

17 Marsh, I (2013) The decline of democratic governance, *The Political Quarterly*, 84 (2). There is a gap/gulf between the political system and its publics, caused by: hollowed out parties, look-alike parties, more pluralized and differentiated publics, more disaffected and volatile publics, centralized celebrity-based politics, market-based and focus-group-driven politics, 24-hour media cycle, short-termism in policy and populism in rhetoric.

18 John, P (2013) Experimentation, behaviour change and public policy, *The Political Quarterly*, 84 (2). How far should the government legislate to enforce, or encourage/'nudge', people to change their behaviours in directions that the government thinks is 'good' for them and for the country? Behaviour change could be more effective/less expensive than 'tax and spend' eg in relation to health services and costs.

19 *Lincoln*, great film directed by Steven Spielberg (2012). Even the greatest moral and political tasks need oiling by tawdry political manoeuvring.

20 *The Confessions of Gordon Brown* – fascinating play by Kevin Toolis (manyriversproductions, 2014). Surmounting the challenges of private and public life and climbing the greasy political pole. Reaching the top piles on fresh frustrations.

21 a The Jury Team (2009) *The End of the Party*, The Jury Team (founded by Sir Paul Judge). Proposes a radical change in the way in which MEPs/MPs are selected so that, in the same way as a jury, they can go back to being independent people exercising their judgement and not just delegates of a political party. 'The current party political

system has turned the UK's Parliament and Government into the creatures of a small and increasingly distant group of oligarchal politicians.'
- **b** The Jury Team (2010) *Working Together for the People Politicians Forgot*, The Jury Team (General Election Policy Document).
22 Various (2009) *The Little Book of Big Expenses: How to live the MP lifestyle*, A & C Black, London
23 Gus O'Donnell (2013) Better government, *The Political Quarterly*, 84 (3) (Gus O'Donnell is the former Head of the Civil Service and Cabinet Secretary). Also, Berry, C and Berry, R (2014) Better the Devil – a response to Gus O'Donnell's 'Better Government', *The Political Quarterly*, 85 (1).
24 Gray, J (2014) The Liberal delusion, *Prospect Magazine*, 23 September. 'As it faces an increasingly disordered world the greatest danger for the West comes from the groundless faith that history is on its side.'

6C.2 Reforming our democratic value chain

Ever-fewer people are joining political parties or voting in elections. Therefore it is increasingly easy for politicians and governments to be controlled by determined and well-off/covertly financed minorities, lobbyists and consultants (consider the United States and the way that Congress is dominated by small numbers of wealthy individuals and lobby groups).

Furthermore, it is not evident that successive UK governments have enhanced the virtues of our democratic system in the eyes of other peoples – have we created more enemies than friends abroad? Of course, we have many diligent and effective constituency MPs. Some ministers and mandarins have achieved substantial progress on our behalf. However, the whole system of government and its members does not operate sufficiently well on our behalf, and we need it to perform substantially better. We need it to produce more net value for us.

We have covered the potential and the problems of some key value chains earlier in this chapter, such as finance, the public sector as a whole, plus health and care, defence and transport. In addition, we are failing to develop cost-effective and secure energy resources, education for all, population number management, including skills and locations and housing. All of these areas and others need the application of modern value chain management by people with the required capabilities.

Further details of governmental failings, as well as opportunities to improve value for all, are given in the Notes.

We could try to improve our democracy by altering the election system from the first past the post system (who wins the most votes in each constituency election) to proportional representation (PR) – seats allocated on the basis of total votes cast for each political party. However, preferably we should adopt truly open primary elections.

a I strongly recommend truly open primary elections held in advance of parliamentary elections, which would not depend so much on the main political parties. These would require each candidate to state and prove their true qualifications for office – that is, their capabilities relevant to the role to be performed (see below). People need to be re-convinced that they are voting for worthwhile candidates. Compare open primary elections very favourably with the closed primaries in the United States, in which only registered Republicans or Democrats may vote – democracy for the wealthy?

b PR would be most likely to result in more hung parliaments and more coalition governments.

c Voting age should be reduced to 16 in order to engage our youth in making democracy work well.

d Compulsory voting will not improve matters while people do not respect politicians and the political process.

e More powers need to be devolved away from Westminster and London to the cities and regions. London is a 'semi-foreign' country with many people working there temporarily to earn a good living before returning to their homelands – they have little interest in the longer-term development of the rest of Britain. The people of Britain need to feel meaningfully closer to their representatives.

f The House of Lords should be restructured into a much smaller and more representative second chamber. Who currently respects the Lords? Proposal: Each of our agreed key national institutions should nominate two members of the second chamber, totalling 50 per cent; political parties should nominate 20 per cent of members: the remaining 30 per cent should be elected by the people. The total membership should not be more than 400. The terms of office should be limited to two times five years. Should only the elected members receive any (modest) recompense?

g Who respects some of the current behaviours in the Commons, as witnessed on TV, notably at Prime Minister's Question Time?

More radical action is needed if we are to have more capable and honest politicians. (Of course, we must recognize that the same could be said of politicians in many democracies.) Naturally an effective politician needs style, but this must be backed by genuine substance. An effective politician needs good 'packaging', but the 'product' must deliver genuine satisfaction to the electorate.

It is evident that too many of the key issues facing our country are not being well defined, analysed and managed through to cost-effective success. Key actions to achieve substantial improvements are believed to be:

1 All persons standing for Parliament, joining a government, or taking up a senior position in the Civil Service or indeed in any important organization, should indicate to the electorate the specific capabilities they possess relevant to their role, eg record of practical success in a valuable role – instituting and running a business, charity or agency; managing a substantial, complex project or programme; tangible success in science, the arts, education, or the law, but not just party politics, PR or the media. Furthermore, continuities in post must match the objectives and timetables. Increasingly, both senior civil servants and government ministers do not remain in post longer than two to three years, and institute half-baked reforms that they will not see to 'fruition', eg health, defence, transport. We now have institutionalized incapability.

2 All major initiatives, projects and programmes should have their objectives, benefits, value chains, costs, plans and timetables, opportunities and risks, management structures, process and data architectures clearly defined in a standard way (see the ensuing Chapters 8 to 12). What outcomes is it intended to deliver to whom, how, when and at what costs? This will help to avoid so many half-baked schemes being launched on political whims. Too many initiatives paint a glowing but vague picture of the benefits and very optimistic estimates of costs (including through-life costs) and timetables. Risks are minimized or ignored. Badly designed political initiatives cannot be redeemed through increasingly complex legislation. Legions of political advisers and tame journalists are no substitute for rigorous analysis and sound implementation structures. We also need to develop effective education in how to calculate accurately and relevantly. Far too many in Parliament and government, including the senior Civil Service (plus the media, the law), come from the same limited educational background, which also suffers from being largely devoid of quantitative skills. In the UK government of 2015, there were no graduates in science and engineering and few senior civil servants have these qualifications.

3 More initiatives, projects and programmes should be run via specifically designed, publicly owned agencies rather than via megalithic government departments or private contractors or consultancies, which too often fail us. Who believes that the Sercos, Capitas, G4Ss, Atoses etc of this world represent value for money, after their failings on such projects as Olympics security and tagging of criminals and numerous IT systems? Our ministers and mandarins do not understand how to procure cost-effectively from the private sector and continue to source from the usual suspects. These new agencies must be staffed by relevantly capable people for necessary periods of time and within appropriate stable budgets.

4 Develop a new, modern, rigorous framework for evaluating the performance of our democracy and its key institutions. The National Audit Office and the parliamentary Select Committees specialize in being wise after the event. The Treasury does not thoroughly understand uncertainty and risk;

for example, it has argued that risks can be positive or negative and that its ownership should be transferred to suppliers via tightly drawn contracts – this regularly fails (eg Private Finance Initiatives, NHS Connecting for Health, Astute submarines and Nimrod aircraft defence projects – see Chapter 11). The responsibilities and accountabilities of ministers need to be re-thought along with their relationship with the Civil Service. This new governance also needs to be applied in the private sector, especially including the financial world.

Politics is the art of preventing people from taking part in affairs which properly concern them. (Paul Valéry)

These proposals were submitted to the Select Committee on Parliamentary and Constitutional Reform and appear on its website. We live in hope.

A review of some modern value chains

6D

VOLUNTARY AND CHARITABLE | SPORT | THE ARTS

6D.1 Voluntary and charitable sector value chains

The United Kingdom would not function as well as it does, and it would be a less attractive place to live, were it not for the voluntary and charitable sectors. So many key activities are undertaken by volunteers and by charities to aid people and places. It could be argued that some of the best-run organizations in the country operate via volunteers and charitable giving. For example, the Royal National Lifeboat Institution and the Hospice Movement are models of service and cost-effectiveness that many other public and private bodies should envy and emulate.

It is believed that there are about 160,000 charities in Britain, and there are many more voluntary bodies which are not formal charities. The annual turnover of charities is about £40 billion. Individual taxpayers contributed around £6.5 billion to charities in 2014, while the government contributed £11 billion.

Nevertheless, voluntary and charitable value chains depend on particular needs being identified, or not, and on volunteers who may continue to give freely of their time and talents, and on donors who are willing to continue giving, and also on central and local government being supportive. There are high degrees of uncertainty surrounding many aspects of these value chains. A few areas of need have many voluntary bodies, while many areas of need lack adequate support, especially in the more deprived parts of the country. While government depends greatly on voluntary and charitable bodies to undertake work which it cannot or will not undertake itself, it has no guarantees that the coverage will be adequate or ongoing. The same applies to these bodies' levels of support from the various levels of government.

Core purpose

To enable individuals and communities to fulfil their defined potentials and to have key needs met, which would otherwise not be realized by market forces nor by the state. To enable individuals and communities to use their talents in the support of 'good causes'.

Strategy

To identify areas of need by people or animals or places. To encourage volunteers to give of their time and talents and donors to provide the required resources. To develop communities of recipients and providers of needed goods and services.

Objectives

1 To define the deserving individuals, animals, places and communities and the needs to be met.
2 To define the required resources, finance, facilities and, vitally, the human capabilities.
3 To recruit and retain the volunteers and the required paid management.
4 To raise funds economically and wisely, and to spend them effectively so that donors are inspired and not demotivated.

Plans

To develop relevant, integrated and motivational plans, focused on the end recipients, across appropriate timescales. To ensure that these plans evolve satisfactorily as circumstances change.

Measures of performance

1. Services delivered to the defined end users, and thereby the outcomes realized.
2. Needs that still require to be met.
3. Revenues and profits generated from voluntary contributions, special fundraising initiatives and from trading. Also grants received. Maximizing the taxation and other benefits from charitable giving, such as via Gift Aid.
4. Costs incurred, including costs of administration and other overheads.
5. Thereby, in relation to points 3 and 4, the margins being realized in relation to the effort involved.
6. Numbers and types and capabilities of volunteers involved.
7. Collaboration with other voluntary organizations and with national and local government.
8. Meeting defined standards of governance. This includes ensuring that a high percentage of surpluses goes to the intended beneficiaries and not inappropriately to overheads or executive salaries.

Analysis

1. Some topics attract too many voluntary organizations and some too few. In many places, it is impossible to discover all the relevant bodies operating within each charitable sector. In other areas, too few voluntary bodies and volunteers exist. A further issue is that some people, and notably the elderly, suffer from several conditions, which makes it difficult to direct them to the best sources of help. In relation to the elderly, and to the poor, and to the mentally ill, the needs continue to increase at the same time as total necessary resources become ever more constrained.
2. Many of the best charities are led by dedicated and charismatic leaders. Succession planning is essential, but can be difficult.

3 Some areas can become over-reliant on professional fundraisers who may take too great a percentage of what is raised.

4 Donors may suffer from 'charitable fatigue' when deluged with demands.

5 Volunteers are not always easy to manage.

6 Sound governance is essential within the framework laid down by the Charity Commission and by auditors. This framework must continue to evolve. Too often it is inadequate.

Reference will be made in particular to Project Mala, which provides schools in one of the poorest parts of India. This was founded in 1989 by Robin Garland MBE, a retired industrialist. SportsAble, which supports handicapped UK athletes, will also be described. It was founded in 1975 and is led by John Jenkins MBE, a retired e-business and supply chain expert. John was disabled by polio at an early age. Nevertheless, he has been a successful businessman, Paralympian and voluntary value chain leader.

The fundamental focus must be on the end beneficiary – who needs what types of care and how these are to be provided in an efficient and effective manner. Management of voluntary and charitable value chains is often more difficult than in other private and public organizations with paid employees. A successful senior businessman once described his frustrations from trying to organize volunteers in a charity bookshop: 'The kind volunteers do not always take kindly to being managed in a disciplined way in order to generate good sales and profits for the charity – after all they are giving their time freely. It is their hobby.'

It is essential to understand the particular value chains well. Where is value added and where is it being lost? Who are the individuals and organizations that could contribute most, not just with money, but also with support and with improved performance?

Project Mala

The head office is in York, UK, but most of the key executives are in India. Mala's core purpose is to provide daytime schooling for children who would otherwise be working all day in the knotted carpet industry. The focus is on remote parts of Uttar Pradesh, which is one of the poorest parts of India. Mala importantly provides schools and teachers in order to ensure a good education for children and a more valuable future for them, their families and the local communities.

This value chain consists of buyers of carpets across the world, sales and marketing, storage, transport, factories, workers, parents and children, food and raw materials suppliers, designers, teachers, suppliers of essentials (such as water, electricity, power, food and clothing, IT), fundraisers in the UK and now across the world, and Indian local government and officials. In essence, the value chain links those across the developed world who want good carpets with families and workshops making carpets in the developing world, while greatly enhancing the education and life prospects of their children.

Project Mala values

Mala was founded in 1989 as an action programme for the elimination of child labour in the hand-knotted carpet industry in Northern India. The industry provides viable employment for adults, and the carpet exporters support the charity in the development of schools to ensure that a progressive education is provided for many children. In addition, adequate nutrition and uniforms are provided. This helps to lift the people and the region out of poverty and to promote economic and social development.

Individuals in the UK and other parts of the world sponsor children and make charitable donations to fund the running of the schools. Project Mala now has ten schools – six primary, three middle schools and one secondary college; 1,300 children are now in full-time education.

Since its foundation, over 7,000 children have benefited from this project. This initiative also provides jobs for 70 teachers, cooks and other people in this rural community.

Many of the poorest areas still have no effective schools. Some districts may have new school buildings, but these are too often unoccupied since there is no integrated system to make them work. Often there are trained teachers, but they may take the pay and not turn up at the school, since they can do a second job for additional pay. Adequate enforcement too often does not exist. In the meantime, some charities like Project Mala work hard to fill the gaps.

Although there have been and are many commitments by Indian national and local governments, international charities, development agencies and by international companies to eliminate child labour, few have had the requisite impact on the carpet community. Some children still have to work to support their family incomes. A recent survey by Project Mala among the children in their schools showed that all children were involved in significant work on household chores to support the family.

The demand for hand-knotted carpets has declined substantially over the past 20 years, partly due to the stigma attached to the use of child labour by Western media. Production has switched mainly to tufted carpets, which are made by injecting wool into a hessian cloth stretched over a frame. The pattern is stencilled on to make production quicker and easier. As this method requires some physical strength to hold the tufting gun, there are fewer jobs for children. However, children still must work after school, mainly in domestic industries which escape the gaze of Western media.

The caste system in India remains strong. Those in the lower castes have lower expectations from life, and indeed lower life expectancy than individuals who are members of the higher castes. In 2005, only 11 per cent of women married outside their caste. Education not only gives lower-caste people abilities in reading, writing and arithmetic, it also gives them confidence to improve their prospects by challenging the unwritten rules that restrict their progress towards a better life.

Sound education not only advances the children of today but also the parents of tomorrow. In 1989, many of the children entering Project Mala schools were already married, in the sense that they were betrothed and would begin to bear children in their teens. Girls are now delaying having families in order to complete their education.

This charitable value chain focuses on the children, who now receive an education which will make them valuable to India, to their local communities and to their families. The child consumers of education in India are linked to the adult users of carpets abroad via a chain of parents, teachers, workers, volunteers and sellers and distributors of carpets. Progressively all parties understand this value chain and the benefits they derive therefrom.

Values

Concern for children, their futures and their exploitation. Their lives can best be improved through them being freed from child labour during school hours in order to develop their knowledge and life skills. Adult workers and their families have to be confident that they can afford to release their children to go to school and still be able to earn enough money to pay for the essentials of life. The children are very likely to work at home after school in order to help the family to survive. How many children in Britain are in a similar situation?

It is clear that Mala is providing great benefit to the pupils in their schools, to the parents and families, to the local communities and potentially to India overall. Clearly one small charity on its own can only set an example of how to add genuine value to people and to society. It is from invaluable acorns that added value oak trees grow. Mala examines its entire value chain in order that all participants benefit, from child to owner of the carpet.

Wider community values

The whole community and indeed society should be involved in voluntary work in order to benefit the recipients and also the supporters – caring for people and providing effective means of care. Charity workers and givers can gain greatly from their participation, especially when they see individuals and the community progress. In parallel, all parties have to be confident that their efforts and their donations will be used well. Some charities become little more than fundraising businesses, losing focus on the end beneficiary. Effective governance is essential. In the UK, the Charity Commission plays a key role in defining and supporting sound practices.

A key issue, which relates particularly to the elderly and the young, is that very often handicaps are multiple. Many charities tend to focus on single handicaps, which can make them less effective for individuals with multiple problems. Twenty per cent of the UK population are disabled (17 per cent from birth and 83 per cent via injury or illness – typically a life-changing condition caused by injury occurs in the age range 17–35, while illness often strikes in the age range 35–48 and again in old age). Too often people suffer from both mental and physical disabilities, which makes it even more difficult to access appropriate support.

Disability is often found within low-income families facing limited opportunities and depending on the benefits system (Figure 6D.1). Disability may result in low self-esteem and low self-confidence. Tackling these issues demands sustained effort on several fronts.

FIGURE 6D.1 A disabled person's value chain

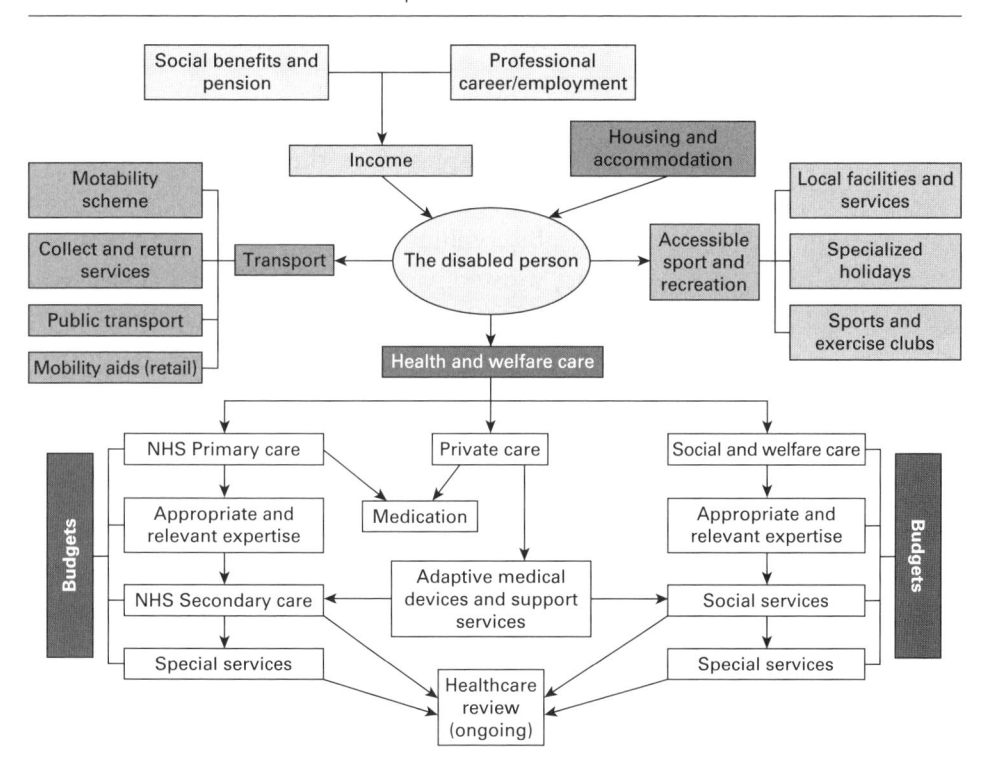

SportsAble Project

The project head office is in Maidenhead, UK. This is a sports club for disabled people with multiple types of disability. The value chain described below links the needs of disabled people with the types of sport, facilities, coaches, managers and fundraisers which are believed to add most value to their lives. SportsAble offers a wide range of different sports to a large community of members (almost 650), around 250 of these being disabled people who participate in sport up to seven days per week. While the club started with very modest facilities and resources in 1975, since then it has developed into one of the most eminent clubs of its type in the UK. It has a very positive national reputation recognized at government level.

The club's focus is grass roots sport, encouraging the disabled person to participate up to the level they desire, whether that be sport for fun or at elite level for Paralympic participation. In simple terms, the value chain links disabled individuals who have a variety of needs, wishes and capabilities with facilities and resources suited to understanding and meeting these. Paying for the facilities and resources involves a team of fundraisers and managers.

SportsAble has a fine track record, having members selected for the GB squad for every Paralympics since the club was formed in 1975, winning medals in each games bar one.

SportsAble is a charitable, voluntary organization employing a small staff team of nine, mostly part-time, in order to run sports seven days a week. The staff undertake the necessary administration from the purpose-built sports complex at Maidenhead, Berkshire. With no central funding, SportsAble has managed, through its own efforts, to raise the £250,000 needed each year to cover its operating costs. Therefore the club is highly dependent on its own fundraising activities and also on local community support, along with the goodwill of its large band of volunteers.

The governance structure of SportsAble is fundamentally important to its undoubted success. It is a registered charity, with a board of trustees/directors responsible for delivering the defined and published objectives (provision of facilities and resources, operation of sports, membership growth, fundraising, generation of work opportunities for disabled people). There is also a trading organization, run by a separate board of directors, which produces funds for the charity. A chief executive officer coordinates the management of both organizations and reports to both boards. There is substantial benefit derived from separating the provision of SportsAble's services from the provision of funding, but ensuring integration at CEO level.

This structure ensures that there is visibly competent management of SportsAble's value chain and that its responsibility to the community is overseen by people recognized as adding community value.

At first sight, the benefits offered to SportsAble's disabled community are obvious. The provision of sport and recreation naturally improves health, and in many cases the enhanced physical capabilities enable greater mobility and improved bodily functionality. Moreover, SportsAble's portfolio of different sports enables the member to focus on the sport that he/she can most enjoy and to compete at the desired level (Paralympic/national/regional/local), thus achieving their *sporting fulfilment*, their aspiration or ambition. However, most members simply want to have some fun via gentle competition. Herein lie the less obvious benefits – the *social fulfilment* – the opportunity to enhance self-confidence, self-esteem and self-worth. These can be truly life-changing benefits. Who is to say that they are not more important than the achievement of sporting success at the highest level?

SportsAble value chain

Individual, family, community, health and care professionals, educational institutions, sports facilities and coaches, disabled transport, fundraisers and events, administration and accounting, Charity Commission and governance, leadership with vision (inspiration and perspiration), local and national government support, charitable trusts with funds, potential participants, volunteers and donors. Never forget the overall community benefit from the visibility of a successful voluntary organization actively helping those in need to enjoy a better life. 'We live in a caring community.'

SportsAble analysis

Developing effective ongoing channels of funding is central to effective voluntary value chains, and is particularly difficult for the handicapped. The disabled are too often in the low-income bracket. The funding for disabled sport at the grass roots level is almost non-existent. Only at the elite level such as Paralympic prospects is funding available via Sports England. All SportsAble's funds have to be generated by the entrepreneurial capabilities of the enterprise business and by the huge efforts of its volunteers and via the local community – never-ceasing hard work:

1 Volunteers have to be found, cherished and managed.
SportsAble is very fortunate to have a large base of volunteers

from all age groups. In order to cope with the churn resulting from natural ageing, fatigue and changing personal priorities, the ongoing recruitment of new volunteers is critical.

2 Awareness has to be fostered at many levels. This very much includes the lack of awareness among the disabled community of the sporting and social benefits on offer. The club employs a marketing manager whose role includes promotion to unaware groups. Social media can help, but their complexities present new and changing challenges.

3 Membership growth is key and has to be managed actively, particularly among youth.

SportsAble values

Participation and fulfilment, both sporting and social. Of course you can. Have a go. Friendship. Volunteering is fulfilling. Active part of the community. Ambition and passion. Facilities and resources to meet many needs. Sound governance. The future can be bright. National recognition.

Overview of voluntary and charitable value chains

Each voluntary body and charitable institution needs to keep defining and monitoring the following:

Core purpose: why does your voluntary body exist? Whom does it benefit? Why should it continue to exist?

Objectives: what outcomes are to be delivered – for and to whom; provided by whom; where and when.

Means: the value chain. How should this work? Do demand and supply balance – often not; why? How should balance be achieved? Costs of provision of an effective service. Sources of funds and costs of fundraising. What other organizations operate in similar areas? Is there duplication or are there gaps? How is collaboration to be enhanced?

Plans: what is going to be done when and by whom? How? What is the net benefit and cost? It is essential to have an agreed development plan which is well publicized and regularly updated.

Measures: numbers of people helped versus numbers needing help. Real outcomes. Administrative costs as a percentage of total income.

Opportunities: given what still needs to be done, for whom, how best to do it. Learning from best practice. What other bodies are or could be active in similar areas, and how is cooperation to be achieved? Learning how to collaborate well.

Risks: the end users may be lost sight of if a charity becomes a pet project for individuals: it can be difficult to manage volunteers who are giving of their own time – special diplomatic skills may be required. Ensure continuity of key management roles.

Governance: carefully follow the Charity Commission guidelines and rules. Build on them to get the controls you need. Appoint knowledgeable and dedicated trustees. Keep sound books of account. Publish regular reports. Consult the service users.

Good luck!

6D.2 Sports club value chain

This is an example taken from a squash club in order to illustrate how amateur sports clubs and similar organizations should structure themselves systematically in order to achieve their valued objectives within a sound governance framework. Clearly, any sports club exists to promote its sport within its community, and sometimes regionally and nationally. This includes consideration of the value chain within which a club operates – players, courts and equipment, training facilities, teams and captains, officials, the sporting rules to be followed, first-aid facilities, the national and regional governing bodies of the sport, spectators, managers, committees, internal and external maintenance staff, juniors and parents, schools, youth clubs, any neighbouring sports, catering and bar staff (essential for generating funds and for replenishing liquid), funding bodies such as Sport England, sponsors, brewers and local authorities. Also, depending on whether you have external trading income, or are part of official playing fields, you can be subject to different reporting and tax implications.

Each such value chain needs to be carefully defined and analysed in order to seek and implement improvement opportunities and also to minimize risks of loss of income, members and valuable contacts.

This particular squash club has around 200 members and operates four modern courts. It is part of a large sports complex and shares a clubhouse with cricket, rugby and tennis. It has players of all ages from 6 to around 80.

Core purpose

To attract people of all ages to play and enjoy squash. To develop fitness and the ability to react quickly: to organize competitions for all via internal mini leagues and club teams; friendships develop well since squash can be very dangerous if players are not aware of each other and are not considerate. Squash usually attracts sound characters.

Values

Fitness in body and mind. Awareness and care about others (people will not play squash with you if you are a danger to others on court – rackets, balls, walls, floors and bodies can hurt). Determination to win well, with some style and fairly.

Objectives

Aim to be the best squash club in the area in order to attract members and also some higher-quality squash players so as to perform well in competitions.

- Providing high-quality courts and facilities.
- Maintaining competitive subscriptions and fees.
- Employing attractive publicity. Communicating well and regularly with value chain partners.
- Ensuring a good atmosphere and effective discipline on and off the court.

Means

Publish a clear and concise constitution and rules for current and potential members. This will include:

- Membership, subscription and fee rules.
- Management committee roles and rules, such as for chairman, secretary, treasurer, development officer, team captains, membership secretary, governance officer, coach – including procedures, terms of office and elections, meetings, accounts, working with external organizations, forward plans.
- Coaching regulations for adults and juniors, including fees, qualifications, background checks. Publish safeguarding rules covering key aspects of potential vulnerability of members.
- Team regulations – which teams are in which leagues. Captaincy and coaching.
- Rules for court use and behaviour on and off court. Disciplinary procedures.
- Governance – adherence to internal and external rules and procedures. In particular, what are the uncertainties, both opportunities and risks, and the corresponding actions?

Publish an integrated development plan to inspire valuable contributions. This will describe the opportunities to be exploited and the risks to be mitigated. Ensure that this is well publicized and regularly updated.

Publish a timetable of events in order to maximize participation.

Opportunities

For example, gain additional members; expand junior section; improve facilities via an affordable rolling programme; enhance value for money; pursue sources of funding; enhance coaching; improve safety and security; improve teams' performances; enhance club's mini leagues; enhance club sports and social events; improve communications with members; enhance the club website; develop use of electronic communications and social media; strengthen relationships with all key partners in your value chain.

Risks

Expenditure, both internal and external, can get out of control. Club subscriptions and charges need to be kept at levels that will attract and not discourage membership. Court availability must be well balanced between individuals, team matches, competitions and coaching. Other squash clubs, or even other sports, can become more attractive. Poor discipline and behaviour can damage the club's reputation. Effective safeguarding of the vulnerable needs to be in place.

Each sports club, and indeed other voluntary body, should define its opportunities and risk as outlined above. Action plans must be written to show who is responsible for doing what and by when. As in all value chains, the membership need to know about and have confidence in what the leadership is doing. Members need nurturing.

6D.3 The arts value chains

Life without the arts would be much less valuable and fulfilling. Value is added at a personal level, a community level, a societal level and, of course, at a commercial level. There are many different arts value chains but they share some common threads which I have woven below.

Core purpose

Encouraging artists to create paintings, sculpture, architecture, interesting environments, music, books, plays and other items that enhance them as individuals, bring pleasure to others and add beauty, interest and value to society.

Objectives

1. Love of producing art. Joy and satisfaction from being creative and from envisioning and then giving birth to the work of art, book, design, building, musical composition, or play. Exhibiting or performing in front of an audience.

2 Love of seeing or hearing art. The sheer enjoyment to be gained from a painting, a sculpture, a fine book, a play, a building or a musical manuscript. Seeing, or hearing, is enjoying. Often, an enjoyment shared is an enjoyment doubled.

3 An investment. An art collection can be a store of value. However, what is true of all investments is even truer for art – an object is only worth what someone will pay for it on a particular day in a particular place. Liquidity does not only apply to water features.

4 Social cachet. Impressing friends and contacts by possessing unique items that 'obviously' cost a lot of money or, more importantly, have great artistic value. On a 'lesser' scale, a good book collection impresses bibliophiles, a stamp collection can impress philatelists, and a coin collection can bring smiles to the faces of numismatists.

5 Completing a series. It is highly satisfying to have a complete collection of: signed first editions of books by a fine author; a series of signed limited-edition prints by a recognized artist; fine porcelain plates or pottery from a great studio.

6 Building a collection which can be donated to a good museum or gallery, or college, or library.

Arts value chains

The arts have many value chains, which differ in structure and content and of course in style. Clearly, the music value chain ultimately aims at a performance heard by people, and with luck some income thereby for the composer and performer. The painting value chain could simply consist of painting or drawing for personal pleasure, but most artists would wish for their works to be exhibited, appreciated and even purchased. Similarly for sculptors and writers (including poets).

Artist/composer/writer/performer/designer; owner; observer/listener (visitor, friend, family, aficionado, paying audience, buyer); gallery/shop/website/concert hall; competitions; auction house; markets; agent/dealer; artist (again); studio; materials and equipment suppliers; framer; printer; art schools; conservatoires; colleges; museums; libraries;

recordings; prints; sources of inspiration (other artists living and dead); sources of talent.

Monetary value is determined in primary and secondary art markets. Primary markets most often involve dealing directly with the artist. The buyer is rarely paying adequately for the time, effort and cost involved in producing the work of art. Talent, originality, skill and ingenuity are most often worth far more, but paid less, than the number of hours spent, pages and canvases created, and the pens, brushes and tubes of paint consumed. There are many more poor (ie impoverished) than rich artists. Does original art depend upon a tortured soul starving in a garret?

On the other hand, without a potential audience and especially a buyer, how much art would be created? It has been rightly observed that beauty lies in the eye of the beholder, since without the eye of the beholder, can there be beauty?

Secondary markets, which usually operate without the artists' presence (they may be dead), are functions of artistic reputation, provenance (proof of authenticity and history of ownership), existence of a catalogue raisonné by a reputable authority, appearance of artist's work in well-known galleries, performance in a theatre or concert hall, scarcity of supply and the reputation of the agent or auction house.

Issues

1 Fakes reduce the value of art when they are discovered, or even suspected. The best art is copied and the buyer must beware. Perhaps the greatest forger of paintings was Han van Meegeren, whose versions of the great masters fooled the experts until he confessed. On the other hand, Picasso said that some of his pictures were fakes because he did not accept that he had produced them while meeting his own standards. There are 'factories' in China that produce fake reproductions to order. Ideally the buyer must be given a certificate of authenticity and/or a valid provenance (history of ownership). The more the uncertainty about authenticity the lower will be the prices paid. *Caveat emptor* – let the buyer beware.

2. The condition of a work of art will substantially affect the price. Expert advice may be required. The book trade is a 'good' example of defined standards – from mint condition, through very good, to 'slightly foxed', to beyond repair. These descriptions were beautifully illustrated by Ronald Searle in his book *Slightly Foxed but Still Desirable: The wicked world of book collecting* (Souvenir Press, 1989). My favourite quote from antiquarian booksellers is 'You should never judge a book by its contents'. A fine cover and binding will add to the value of a book, just as a poor frame and discolouration will diminish the value of a painting. As Robert Burns wrote in 'The Book-Worms', 'Through and through th'inspired leaves / Ye maggots, make your windings. / But O respect His Lordship's taste / And spare the golden bindings.'

3. Commissions charged by agents, auction houses and galleries. These can vary wildly from 5 per cent to 50 per cent. One of the best early developments of auctions for both paintings and books was in the Low Countries in the 16th century. Early auctions were based on prices being reduced until someone called out 'Mine', that is, mining auctions, now called Dutch auctions. Book auctions became an important way for publishers to sell books. In the last quarter of the 17th century, over a hundred auctions were held in England, selling 350,000 works and realizing about £250,000.

4. Short-term fashion. Ideally a great work of art will combine a subject of interest, an original style and a sound technique allied with a feeling of being special. Too often modern works of art and music appear to be triumphs of originality/fashion/technology over creative beauty based on sound technique and over sustainable content and interest. I remember seeing the bare brick wall revealed at the Reform Club when a painting was removed for restoration. A wag hung a notice on the bricks saying 'On loan from Tate Modern'.

5. There are myriads of fragmented markets, each with different attitudes to value. Finding and understanding these markets may take as much if not more time than creating the work of

art. Antiques and their values now form the subject of many TV programmes, which are entertaining and often enlightening. But do not underestimate how much effort may be involved in finding the best and most trustworthy market for your work of art. Some works of art may even be dissected to produce others, for example collages or floor 'sculptures'. I was saddened to hear from a London shop that sells framed photographs of famous people with their signatures that an autographed copy of a book by such an individual would have the signature cut from the book and inserted into the picture frame – sadly, the autographed photograph can be worth more than the book, and also easier to sell.

6 In a number of arts value chains, competitions play an important role in gaining recognition and adding value. For example, the Leeds, Chopin and Tchaikovsky piano competitions are very important to the careers of pianists; the Turner Prize is of great significance to modern artists; the Man Booker Prize is highly sought after by novelists.

Most of us are sufficiently fortunate to have hobbies and recreations. We place great value on these, without usually calculating their values in monetary terms. We value but do not price the time we spend on our hobbies. Particularly interesting collections of paintings, books, coins or musical instruments will usually be valued, notably for insurance purposes. The most important items will need to be valued at the death of the owner.

Beware of leaving your inheritors to value your treasured possessions after your passing – take action in advance of the last trumpet.

We should particularly think afresh about our arts value chains in order to improve their contributions, current and potential, to society and also to the creative artists. The arts and their value chains help greatly to civilize us.

A question of identity

07

Introduction

We have all become used to barcodes in supermarkets. We are confident that the checkout scanner will link the item we are buying to a computerized list of prices and charge us correctly. The item will be accurately identified and any discounts and multi-buys will be precisely applied. When we pay by debit or credit card we believe that our card and personal identification number (PIN) will access only our own bank and bank account, and transfer only the correct amount of money to this particular retailer.

How did these agreed and dependable systems of identification come into operation? How can all these data be made available wherever they are needed? If we can achieve this correct identification in shops, how can we also correctly identify patients, diagnoses, treatments and drugs in hospitals and clinics?

Similarly, how can we know at each airport in the world exactly what spare parts a particular aircraft requires, where that part can be sourced and how each part should be fitted?

Having achieved so much in correctly identifying items and people, what key problems of identification remain, particularly in relation to us as individuals? Why is so much of our personal data badly organized when held in systems that are supposed to support us when we need to call on national and local government resources and on the private sector? Why are we poorly identified when we most need help? I shall now provide answers to these questions. It is a question of identity.

Within this chapter I shall touch on a number of organizations vital to the development of identification technology, bodies to which I wish to declare my affiliation. I am an honorary life member of both GS1 (Global Standards 1) and UKCeb (UK Council for Electronic Business), having been closely involved with the early development of their systems and processes. I was also intimately involved in the development of the e-business standard, addressed in detail in the section on electronic business below; here I chaired the TRADACOMS standards group and oversaw the TRADANET tender and development process. I also led the introduction of a global UN standard for e-business communications as Head of the UK Delegation for Trade Facilitation and Electronic business to the UN in Geneva.

Barcodes

Consider a jar of Nescafé Gold Blend coffee with a scannable symbol, a barcode, on its back. Its number is 50 00243 969107. This number is represented by a symbol that can be scanned by a laser beam at a shop checkout. The checkout is linked to a computer in an office in the store and this number of this particular jar of Gold Blend is looked up on a list of products and prices. This information is then communicated back to the checkout and Gold Blend 200 gram and its price are printed on your till receipt.

It was on 25 June 1974 that the first product was scanned in a supermarket in Troy, Ohio as a result of the pioneering efforts of Alan Haberman. He called this system the Universal Product Code. When this system came across to the UK from the United States in the mid-1970s, marketing brand managers were aghast that their beautiful packaging was being wrecked by these ugly black and white symbols. However, retailers and manufacturers soon agreed that it was to the consumer's benefit to have quick and accurate pricing at the checkout. It was also to everyone's benefit thereby to be able to measure rates of sale of each product immediately and then to restock each shop accurately and promptly.

The number on each product is defined within the International Article Number System (EAN), now called the Global Trade

Identification Number (GTIN). This is a 13-digit code – the first two digits define the country number bank that issued that number (50 is the UK, run by a body now named GS1 (Global Standards 1) in London). The next five digits define which company owns the product. These first seven digits do not necessarily tell you who made the product or where it was made, but simply who owns the number. The last five digits define the individual product pack – 200 gram jar of Nescafé Gold Blend. Each product pack number is unique and also meaningless. You can only find out information about the pack by linking the number to a computer file containing: its description – size of pack, type of coffee (or tea or jam); is it a single jar, or is it a multipack, or is it in a case of 24 or 48, or in a pallet or container? The reason for doing things this way is that it is easier to change information on a computer file than to change the number and symbol on each item every time you alter the information about the item, for example if salt has been omitted from the ingredients or the weight has changed.

If the barcode is on a bottle of French beer, a laser beam immediately recognizes and generates the right number. In addition to its remarkable accuracy, these barcode symbols are simple and cheap to apply to all shapes and sizes of product. There is very little effect on the cost of packaging, and scanning the symbol does not affect the speed of production or distribution. On a high-speed line in a factory or in a distribution depot, the same identity can be used to count cases or to route them automatically to different points in the building.

Master data

So we now know how to recognize the number of each product pack. How do we get all the other information we need to know about it? This information is called master data, which include such facts as the detailed description of the product, its weight, its price to the consumer depending on whether it is being sold singly or as part of a multi-buy (eg three for the price of two, any four bars for £1), its detailed description, its ingredients if relevant (eg contains nuts, gluten free). Such data are nowadays very important to both retailers and consumers. Wrong data can seriously affect health. Think then about how vital accurate data are when applied to a life-saving drug, or to a strong poison. It can be a matter of life and death.

The best source of accurate data about a product is from the originator, usually the manufacturer. The manufacturer has to confirm with the retailer not only the key ingredients, but also the prices to be charged by the manufacturer to the retailer for the different traded units – the retailer orders the products it needs in cases or pallets, not in single consumer units.

How is all this information to be exchanged in an accurate, timely and low-cost manner?

Electronic business

The solution was to develop electronic business – computer-to-computer exchange of all information that needs to be shared by customers and suppliers. In the 1970s, it was impractical to communicate computer to computer. The relatively impractical alternative was to try to agree a common standard for magnetic tape (like a large reel of film) and to send these tapes via a motor cycle courier.

In the later 1970s, major retailers were beginning to demand that their suppliers send invoices on magnetic tape in order to reduce errors and processing costs. One key problem was that each retailer wanted a different electronic format, because each had different computers, systems and processes. This variety of formats would have been very complex and costly to achieve. So, in order to agree a common standard, a group was set up by the suppliers and retailers to define this single standard for invoices and orders, as well as for the master data on products, prices and other trading information.

Defining an e-business standard involves the same steps as developing a spoken language. You need to agree what words are to be used and precisely what each word means, that is, a data dictionary. You also must agree the rules for combining words into sentences or messages, that is, the grammar or syntax. Then you must define the messages – the order, the invoice and the payment. Only then do you specify the technical means of exchanging the messages between customers and suppliers – via a private electronic network or via the internet. Getting competing businesses to agree common standards was, and is, like herding cats. Remember that standards are like toothbrushes – everyone knows you have to have one, but no one wants to use someone else's.

It was also important that the government be persuaded to make electronic invoicing legal. Until the Finance Act of 1980, only paper invoices were accepted by a court of law. Britain was one of the first countries in the world to replace paper with electronic invoicing, and produced its first agreed and tested Trading Data Communications Standard in 1982. The TRADACOMS standard principles and key practices remain in use today in the FMCG industry, since they are based on agreed simple and standard business processes, such as 'an order is for the delivery of one or more items to one place on one date', since a delivery can only be in practice of 'one or more items to one place on one date' (see Chapter 8). For example, when you place an order you ask for specific quantities of the products you want to be delivered to your address on a specific day. You then confirm that the physical delivery consists of the specified items to your defined location on the agreed date. Thereby an invoice should relate precisely to each such confirmed delivery and back to the original order. For this structured process to work, products, customers and suppliers must be uniquely identified. Therefore each trading location also has its own GTIN code.

The United Nations in Geneva was later persuaded to adopt these principles (named Simpl.e.business) for electronic business and trade facilitation across the world. Remember that major delays occur in importing and exporting if goods arrive at a frontier Customs post before the necessary documentation, and if the documentation is not accurate. Electronic business according to agreed standards ensures that accurate documentation and products arrive at the right time for prompt Customs post and port clearance.

Once a standard order to deliver goods to a specific place had been agreed, the same principles were applied to ordering goods to be produced, or payments to be made via a bank, or materials to be processed in a factory, or patients to be treated by a doctor. Indeed, when one adds unique IDs for people, treatment processes and the assets involved, for example, the order can be from a doctor to a consultant radiologist to scan a particular patient using an agreed process or procedure using a particular asset or device (X-ray machine or a CAT scanner). I shall return to the topic of health shortly.

Having agreed the TRADACOMS standards, the next step was the development of an electronic method for communicating messages speedily, accurately, securely and at a low cost. In the United States in the early 1980s, one could send orders and invoices to a trading partner via an IBM mainframe computer at a very high charge of up to 50 pence per 1,000 characters. A working party comprised of representatives from Rowntree Mackintosh, Nestlé, Cadbury, Unilever, Tesco, Woolworth and Sainsbury designed a computer network specifically for electronic data interchange, called TRADANET. One requirement was that the cost of using this network should be about 3.5 pence per 1,000 characters instead of 50 pence.

After going out for tenders (17 were received from across the world), the TRADANET network was built and operated by International Computers Ltd (ICL). The ICL team was run by Christopher Gent, who in later life became Sir Christopher Gent and went on to be chairman of Vodafone.

In April 1985, the first live test of the network was conducted. This involved each of the small number of manufacturers and retailers sending an order and an invoice to each other's electronic postbox and then retrieving the corresponding messages from their own electronic mailboxes. Unlike far too many new computer systems, this worked first time – due to the great capability and commitment of all those involved. TRADANET went from strength to strength thereafter and was copied in many parts of the world. Later the service was run by GXS.

Note in particular the high degree of security built into TRADANET. You can only receive agreed standard messages via secure electronic postboxes and mailboxes from businesses that you know and trust. Compare this with the internet, where messages can appear on your computer from anywhere in the word in a multitude of formats. The internet was developed at CERN, near Geneva, to aid communications among many scientists and engineers who trusted each other. The World Wide Web's founder Tim Berners-Lee said later: 'The Web was originally conceived as a tool for researchers who trusted one another implicitly; strong models of security were not built in. We have been living with the consequences ever since.'

In brief, the history of e-business is:

1970s: Barcodes designed and applied, with retailers using their own data about products.

1980s: Electronic data interchange/e-business developed to share product data electronically and also to exchange orders, invoices and payments.

1990s: Development of the internet to connect everyone everywhere. Also, e-exchanges appeared to support the trading of food, fuel, chemicals and so on.

2000s: Direct electronic links to consumers, including home shopping. E-mail abounds. Now we also have social media. People can quickly communicate ideas and comments – some of it helpful and some even accurate.

Banking

We have now established that modern business demands agreed common standards in order to uniquely recognize items, businesses, locations, individuals, processes and assets. These unique identities can be recognized automatically by laser scanners, or by radio waves or by magnetic devices. All the information about these items, locations, individuals and so on are held on computer files which are accessed automatically, and which are kept up to date and secure by the organizations involved.

The same principles are involved in banking. When paying money, for example at the checkout or online, it is even more important that the right sum moves from my account or yours via each of our banks. Every bank has a unique six-digit number, such as 66-77-88. Each of our bank accounts has a unique 8-digit number, such as 66667777. You have an electronically enabled card to access each of your bank accounts with your own personal identification number (PIN).

This greatly enhances security, since electronic bank fraud is always potentially a great problem. The banks have sound systems for transferring money between them – BACS for the UK and SWIFT for international payments.

Electronic tags and RFID

Automatic identification systems started with scannable barcodes and laser beams. On your bank card is an electronic chip, which links to your PIN number. Such chips or electronic tags are now used on many more valuable items such as parcels or container loads of goods. Sometimes criminals are electronically tagged to track where they are. The latest tags may often be radio frequency ID tags (RFID), which can be scanned at some distance by radio waves. In this way a particular order can be tracked across the world as it passes on and off ships, aircraft and lorries. This also involves the use of satellite communications so that containers and shipments can be tracked en route to ports, stores and final destinations. Even newer electronic ID systems include quick response (QR) codes which, when scanned by a mobile phone or webcam, will link through to a website. Additional data can also be contained within a QR symbol, but the more data encoded the bigger the symbol becomes.

Healthcare identification

We have now agreed on the great importance of accurate identification of items and payments and also of the ability to link these IDs precisely and securely to the related files of computer data. What about patients?

At present, we have many different and too often inadequate computer systems in the UK health value chain, including both the NHS and the private sector. We also still have too much paper, some of it inaccurate, some dangerously so. For example, in many hospitals, paper drug charts only have sufficient rows to cover about two weeks' treatment and then they have to be rewritten. Transcribing data introduces errors. The medical correspondent of the *Financial Times* estimated that in 2013, in Yorkshire, 14 per cent of hospital patients experienced medication errors. Surgical errors, therapy errors and so on can result from the inaccurate identification of patients, diagnoses, treatments, clinicians and the availability of the correct drugs (and equipment) in the correct doses at the correct times and places. The key health value chain has to identify accurately the following factors: you must be able to link correctly the patient to the clinician to the diagnosis to the treatment to the drugs or surgical instruments. You also need to be able to order the correct drug and equipment from the manufacturer or supplier and have these delivered without error to the hospital pharmacy and then to the ward or operating theatre and finally to the right patient.

In order for this to be achieved, GS1 is working with the NHS and the pharmaceutical industry to apply the GTIN numbering systems across the health value chain.

Building and maintaining aircraft

Just as each individual is unique, so is each aircraft. Modern aircraft are not designed and built in one place by one company. A Boeing 777 or an Airbus 380 or a Joint Strike Fighter contains components from many parts of the world. These are designed by specialist engineers in facilities in many places and countries linked by electronic communications. This can only be done accurately and securely if agreed standards are used, for example the International Standards Organization Standard for the Exchange of Product Model Data (ISO STEP). In the UK, such standards are supervised by the UK Council for Electronic Business (UKCeb).

The stages in the life of a modern aircraft are:

- Concept development and then detailed engineering design, including simulated construction and flying. This involves the use of virtual reality imaging, simulating the operation of the aircraft on the ground as if it were really being flown. Each individual component is given its own ID, and related master data are developed about its make-up and use.

- One of the most vital components of a modern aircraft is computer software – called embedded software. Approximately 25 per cent of the cost of a plane today is software, and about 90 per cent of that cost relates to what has to happen automatically if something goes wrong – a component stops working, or there is a fire or an engine failure.

- Construction of all the main parts of the aircraft, such as fuselage, wings, controls, engines, again in many different places, all linked electronically.

- Assembly into the complete aircraft in one location, which may only take a matter of days, but can only be achieved if every component of every part of every sub-assembly has been correctly identified and tested to agreed standards.

- Testing and certification of the full aircraft on the ground and in flight.

- Operating the aircraft all over the world. If a plane is flying from London to Sydney via Singapore and a repair is necessary, the detailed electronic records of that particular plane have to be available in each airport so that the precise methods of repair and the correct spares are used. Remember that over the life of an aircraft, many repairs and modifications will be made, which means that no two aircraft are the same – unlike jars of Gold Blend.

The same is true for ships and for all major engineering equipment, whether it is an aircraft carrier or a destroyer. The key sub-assemblies for 21st-century Royal Navy carriers and destroyers were built in various locations and then transported by sea to Rosyth for two aircraft carriers and to Glasgow for six Type 45 destroyers for final assembly and testing.

Modern equipment is increasingly fitted with many sensors to check that all components and systems are operating well and to send signals immediately to base when something starts to go wrong, in order that likely consequences are predicted quickly and contingency actions taken promptly.

Defence

The picture gets even more complex when it comes to overall defence operations. Not only do military operations involve aircraft, ships, vehicles and their crews, but all have to be serviced with food, fuel, ammunition and spares, usually far from their home bases. All have to be able to communicate electronically with each other, with their bases and with military headquarters. Even more difficult to identify is which plane or ship or vehicle is ours, an ally's, a neutral's or an enemy's. But such accurate identification and communication is a matter of life and death.

In the modern world, all computer systems have also to be protected from cyber-attacks. These attacks on systems and data may come from enemy armed forces, foreign governments, industrial competitors or amateur hackers.

A better future for us all

All this may seem a long way from barcodes on groceries in shops. But the same principles need to be followed:

- Who needs to be identified and why?
- What needs to be identified and why?
- What data need to be available about each of these identified people and products and organizations, where and when, across the value chain?
- How are data to be provided, and kept up to date and secure?
- Who needs to communicate that data to whom, and how?
- What standards are to be used?

An effective modern value chain that aims to meet our needs should have the following characteristics:

a Focus on the end user, whether he or she is the shopper, the soldier or the patient – what service does he or she need?

b Define all the participants in the value chain who need to work together to service the end user well. Agree the collaborative processes for efficient working.

c Define the net value to be added by each participant and at what cost.

d Define all the accurate IDs of items, people and places.

e Agree the data and the messages to be shared.

f Develop secure standard electronic communications.

Unfortunately, in reality we are too often faced with 'the silo syndrome' – each department or function in each separate organization behaves as if it is a silo looking after only its own operations – it is not efficiently 'joined up' with the other departments and organizations. For example, in the health industry, and not just in Britain, there are many potential silos – GPs, various types of hospital consultants, therapists, laboratories, nurses, midwives, dieticians, psychiatrists, psychologists, administrators and the Department of Health (plus NHS England, Scotland and Wales, plus Clinical Commissioning Groups – see Chapter 6B on the health value chain). Is the patient consistently the real focus of them all, or too often do people focus largely on the operation of their own individual function – after all, they have targets to meet? For example, many elderly people go into hospital malnourished. Many leave hospital in a poor dietary condition, because too often no one takes effective responsibility for ensuring that a particular patient actually eats the particular food that is necessary for their health.

Identify us well

One of the key problems that faces all of us is that we have too many identities which are supposed to support our dealings with the rest of the world accurately, securely and economically. For example, we have National Insurance numbers, NHS numbers, voter registration, driver and TV licence numbers, banking numbers. We are recognized differently by central and local government and by each department within. For many years we have been debating whether we should have national identity cards. Opponents say this would be an infringement of personal liberty. Government departments could possibly link our data to develop a 'Big Brother' state. The opposing practical argument is that all of us need to be identified correctly, not simply by one government ID card but by joined-up and integrated systems that serve us well, accurately and cost-effectively as citizens. A key issue is often less being identified by the government, but rather government incompetence in designing and running computer systems. For example, the CRB (Criminal Records Bureau, also called the Disclosure and Barring Service) system does not provide a single database indicating all people who are cleared to work with vulnerable children and adults and also all people who are not so cleared. I sit on mental health appeal panels and I have had to receive numerous CRB clearances at substantial effort and cost, including three for the same building because it was providing three different services. At present, we are poorly identified across many national and local government systems and not well served at many crucial times. The results of this are exemplified in the case study presented below.

> The elderly are particularly affected by this as they can have multiple ailments and a diversity of care needs. At the same time, they have difficulty in accessing services and in understanding official communications, especially when these do not recognize them as one unique individual. One elderly lady in York, who had experienced several strokes and therefore found understanding and communicating difficult, fell and cracked her hip. The NHS hospital set the hip and released her into a council care home, since she required further rehabilitation and support. One part of the council runs the home and another part accounts and charges for it. The lady then moved to a new housing association property, since it had been agreed by her, her relatives, her friends and the council that she should sell her own home in order to have more appropriate facilities and support. The council systems did not recognize that it was the same lady who had been admitted to their care home and to the housing association flat, and had vacated her owned address. Even worse, although this lady was receiving home care in the housing association property from a private firm, for which she pays, with the payment being channelled via the council, this part of the council

does not identify her as the same person who has paid and continues to pay council tax. This lady moved to her housing association accommodation a couple of weeks before the end of March 2011, and therefore owed about £100 in council tax for 2010/11. By the time the council had agreed to issue a direct debit form so that money could be transferred to them without the lady needing to take action herself, the council had issued a summons for her to appear in court for non-payment of council tax. At this time the council owed her substantially more than £100 for overpayment for home care. While not every computer system can and should be integrated, we, and especially the elderly, should be identified accurately and consistently across the key organizations and value chains that exist to support us. The most vulnerable individuals must be flagged accordingly across all relevant and related public systems.

Since we are all going to spend more time and effort trying to get information, care and support from ever more complex, under-resourced and too often badly organized central and local government bodies, and also from the private sector and from voluntary bodies, we do now need to develop clearer, simpler procedures and care pathways (value chains) for those who need help. This involves accurate, consistent and linked identification of individuals and the related data about them. This information also has to be confidential and secure. I believe we can and must do much better, and that it can be done at a lower total cost. I shall endeavour to achieve this with friends, colleagues and hopefully with our lords and masters. We must develop sound, focused and cost-effective value chain processes and their necessary data to serve us all.

After all, we all matter – and therefore our identities and data really matter too.

A version of this chapter originally appeared in a speech I delivered at the Harrogate International Festival in 2011.

Constructing sound value chain process and data architectures

08

Including the fundamental value chain process – from plan to payment

Introduction

Once the objectives of any organization, be it private or public, have been agreed, it is essential to define: the internal and external value chain processes; and the supporting data by means of which the objectives will be achieved.

This chapter indicates how these processes should be defined, and also how the process architecture should be well enabled by a data architecture. In an ideal world, these architectures can and should be simple, standard, speedy, certain, safe and secure. These characteristics should be inbuilt. However, these architectures in practice also need to allow for uncertainty and for unexpected events, for doing business beyond the normal value chain as well as for the regular flow of well-structured activities.

Individuals and public and private organizations too often need to deal with sub-optimal decisions by others. These may take the form of badly designed legislation, business plans, targets and reorganizations, threats and ill-considered processes, data and computer systems. Too often, tinkering with one part of a value chain from a blinkered perspective results in extra costs to many participants in the overall value chain and in widespread disappointment with real outcomes. Since very few value chains operate entirely within one organization, one industry or even within one country, a cost-effective, simple and standard global perspective on value is highly desirable, supported by a well-structured framework for analysis, design and implementation.

Structuring the process architecture

It is vital for the value chain participants that key objectives are realistic, meaningful, clearly understood, and translated into shared simple and standard business processes. In turn, this process architecture needs to be supported by an agreed data architecture in order to facilitate fast and unambiguous communication, as well as enabling prompt processing, analysis and implementation of messages and information. Speed, certainty and low total cost of value chain operations need to be supported by the simplification and standardization of both processes and data. This approach will help facilitate the cost-effective application of electronic systems, which, in turn, can significantly enhance speed, certainty, safety and security – a 'virtuous cycle'.

Business processes involve:

1 Participants (customers, suppliers, individuals, teams and functions, both internal and external).

2 Items (products and services).

3 Locations (factories, depots, offices, outlets).

4 Activities (events, actions, conversions from one state to another) include planning, ordering, delivering, invoicing, paying and accounting. The formal description of how an activity is to be undertaken is described in a procedure.

5 Documents provide an agreed record of activities. Documents include the order, delivery note, invoice and payment advice.

6 Assets (facilities, plant and equipment).

7 Resources (financial and material).

Existing processes need to be mapped in order to indicate not only what is achieved where, by whom and with what resources, but also where there are problems of performance, cost and timeliness. Practical improvements then need to be designed, agreed and tested.

Figure 8.1 provides an example of multi-level business process mapping. Systematic and effective improvements cannot be made unless there are relevant, accurate and timely data. Figures 8.2 and 8.3 outline role models which indicate examples of what data need to be shared by whom, and when, in order for customers and suppliers to plan cost-effective joint value chain operations.

In order to indicate how all this work should be done, the most fundamental and widespread of all value chain processes will now be analysed – the plan to payment process.

The plan to payment process

Objectives are realized by implementing a defined plan. Each action or activity that realizes the plan is most often driven by an order to do something:

- Activities(such as supplying a tonne of a particular soap powder) are initiated via orders which have pre-agreed prices (or costs) for each item (product or service) contained within them or related to them in a defined file.
- Orders are then fulfilled by deliveries of items or services, to a particular location on a defined date. The supplier provides a delivery note to accompany the delivery, and this is confirmed (or amended) by the customer

FIGURE 8.1 Objectives to plan to payment

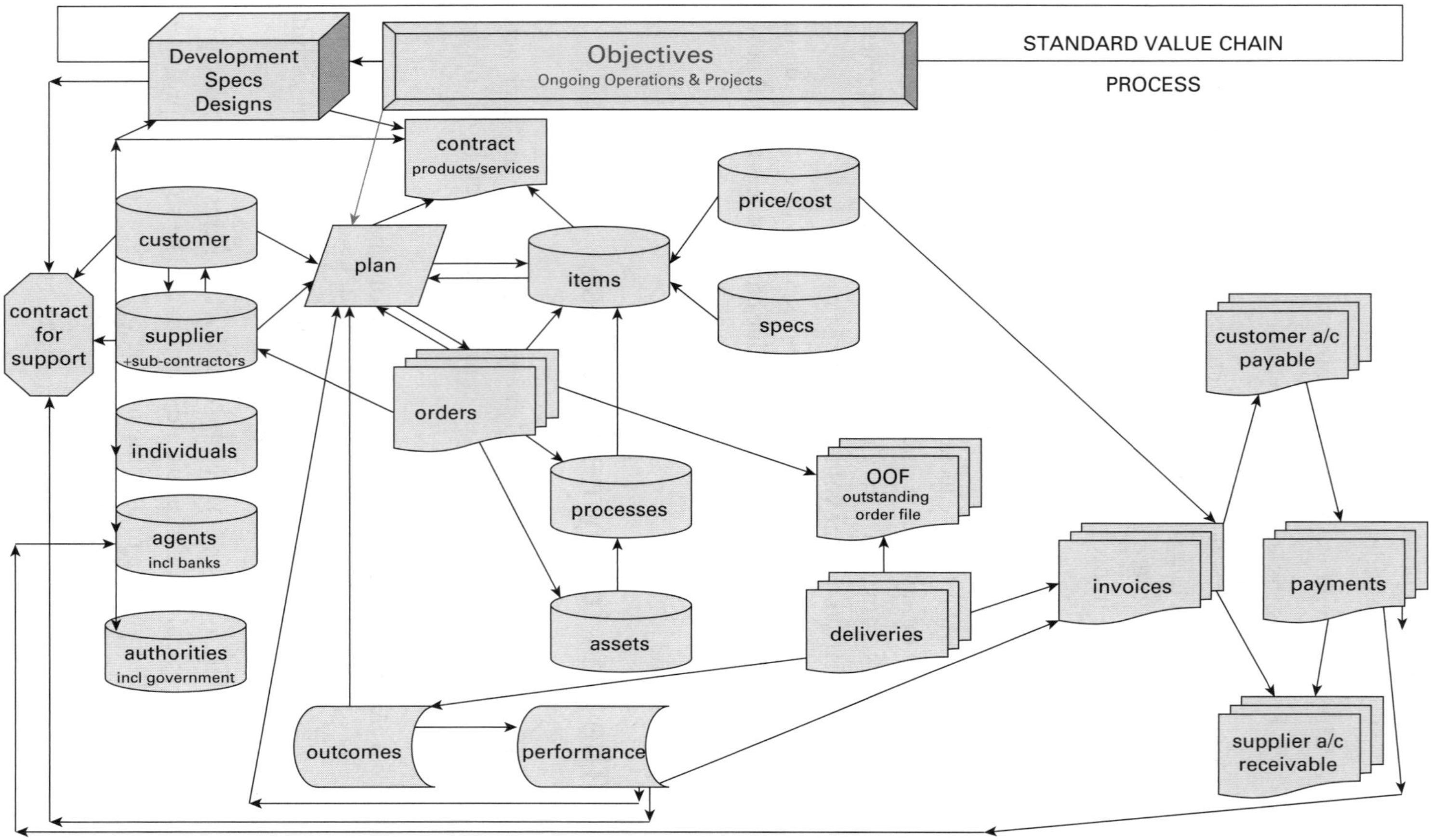

Constructing Sound Value Chain Process and Data Architectures

(Opposite) **Figure 8.1 Note**

Objectives will relate to – 1. Ongoing value chain operations (provision of items and services, or support). Both will often have related contracts, and certainly should have plans agreed between customer and supplier. In the case of ongoing support, the orders will go from the supplier to sub-contractors, rather than from the original customer, who, however, may well want to keep track of key transactions, and certainly of performance.

2. Major projects (for new items and services, and for key changes to the value chain). Again the value chain is largely driven by Objectives → Plans → Orders → Delivery/Performance → Invoice → Payment. The more that all these processes are driven consistently and in a standard way (supported by a standard data architecture based on the Simpl.e.business standards) the better. Simplicity and standardisation across the value chain lead to speed and certainty and low total cost, as well as to safety and security.

Each activity that realises a plan is most often driven by an order from a customer to a supplier to do something. Activities are initiated by orders, which will have pre-agreed prices (or costs) for each product or service (items) contained within. Details of prices/costs and specifications are accessed from master data files. Orders are then fulfilled by deliveries of products or services. Invoices record valid deliveries, and they trigger payments. Accounting systems record current and predicted payments and receivables, and thereby monitor cash flows.

Performance against plans is recorded within dynamic data files.

FIGURE 8.2 Customer–supplier role model for joint value chain management

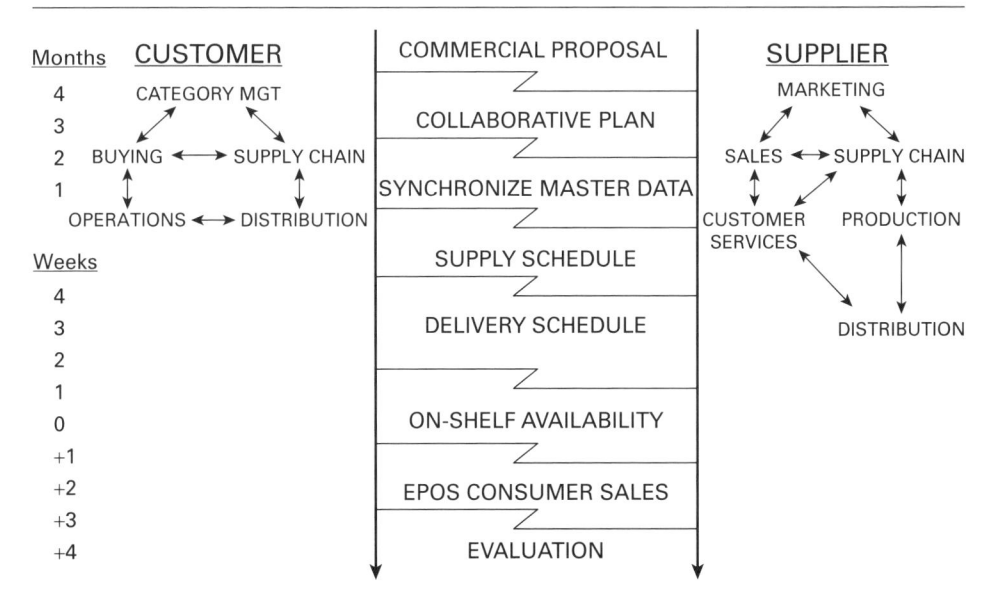

Months	CUSTOMER	COMMERCIAL PROPOSAL	SUPPLIER
4	CATEGORY MGT		MARKETING
3		COLLABORATIVE PLAN	
2	BUYING ↔ SUPPLY CHAIN		SALES ↔ SUPPLY CHAIN
1		SYNCHRONIZE MASTER DATA	
	OPERATIONS ↔ DISTRIBUTION		CUSTOMER SERVICES PRODUCTION
Weeks		SUPPLY SCHEDULE	
4			
3		DELIVERY SCHEDULE	DISTRIBUTION
2			
1			
0		ON-SHELF AVAILABILITY	
+1			
+2		EPOS CONSUMER SALES	
+3			
+4		EVALUATION	

In this example, the key objective is to launch a new product on Date 0. Therefore, months ahead, data have to be shared and agreements reached, not only between the customer and supplier companies, but also within and between all the relevant functions of both businesses. Data have to mean the same to both businesses and therefore to be synchronized and integrated between and within both computer systems. This requires agreed business procedures and data standards ie integrated and standardized process and data architectures.

Data continue to be collected and exchanged after Date 0 in order to measure performance against objectives and to amend actions accordingly.

Building Effective Value Chains

FIGURE 8.3 Role model for VC communications

	Customer Functions						Supplier Functions				Other Agencies
	Marketing	Operations	Distribution	Supply chain	Buying		Sales	Supply chain	Marketing	Production	Purchasing
4 months											
3	✓				✓	✓ Provisional Plan (Internet)	✓	✓	✓		
2					✓	✓ Master Data Synch (EDI)	✓	✓			
						Production/Supply Plan	✓		✓	✓	
1			✓	✓	✓	Delivery Schedules (EDI)	✓				
4 weeks											
3											
2											
1											
7 days											
6											
5				✓		Delivery Orders (ED)	✓	✓		✓	✓
4											
3											
2											
1											
0		✓				Consumer Sale		✓			
+1		✓		✓	✓	EPOS Analysis (Internet)	✓	✓	✓	✓	✓
+2											
+3				✓		Invoices (EDI)	✓	✓			
...		✓	✓	✓	✓	Evaluation (Internet)					

This version of the role model indicates which functions in both businesses will receive and action each type of data.

- Invoices record the valid deliveries at the agreed prices, and they trigger the payment.
- Accounting systems record current and predicted payables and receivables, and thereby monitor cash flows – see Figure 8.4 on the plan to payment process.

An order can be to deliver a product or to provide a service, to design and to make a product, to move an item, to process a material, to treat a patient, to meet an end user's request, to make a payment and so on. An order should be in the form of an instruction from a customer (eg a buyer) to a supplier (eg a seller) to deliver one or more items to one place on one date/time. This is because the delivery of an item or service can only be to one place at one specified time or period. Each invoice should relate to a specific delivery. Payment will relate to the total sum due from one or more specific invoices recorded in a statement of account.

Where there is effective joint management of a value chain, there can be valuable variations on the above theme. Thus:

- Under co-managed inventory, where the supplier and the customer jointly manage stocks on an agreed basis, a supplier may initiate the delivery and by implication the order, and provide a periodic summary e-invoice.
- Under self-billing, the customer may generate the invoice on agreed terms in relation to confirmed deliveries.
- Under through-life support, the supplier or prime contractor may initiate most of the transactions via agreed procedures, providing an audit trail to support the monitoring of performance and the making of payments by the customer.

In all such cases, it is even more important that there are standard agreed processes and data in order to ensure accurate and timely transparency across the value chain. This extends from the end user, through the contracting customer, through formal prime and sub-contractors, through third-party suppliers, through intermediate agents and through official authorities. Clearly, no one needs to know everything; but what needs to be known by whom must be understood and provided accordingly. Effective governance requires there to be a sound audit trail which can confirm compliance.

By following the above process, both customers and suppliers can be clear about the relationship of each order to the plan, of each delivery to an order, of each invoice to a delivery and of each payment to one or more invoices. Measures of performance are thereby clear. In addition, this approach will provide rigorous cross-referencing of payment, invoice, delivery and order transactions to each other, to the plan and to the accounting systems.

All value chain participants will gain benefits by structuring both their internal systems and their shared communications accordingly. For example, a customer who issues orders to suppliers in the form of specified single deliveries to each location on each date is best prepared to match order confirmations, deliveries and invoices with orders. Customers create difficulties for themselves if they issue orders for multiple deliveries to a variety of locations on various dates, and leave the supplier to restructure the message and then confirm their ability to meet what they think has been ordered. The potential problems are compounded if there is no rigorous system for identifying and coding items and locations – see the section on defining a sound data architecture below.

It is valuable to recognize that a plan is simply an intention to place future orders to act, and that outcomes/actuals are the record of the fulfilment of past orders. When all the transactions and data which are related to plans to order, to orders and to outcomes are structured in this rigorous and consistent way, all systems and communications across the value chain become faster, more certain and lower cost because they are less prone to error and are easier to process and action.

Defining a sound data architecture

It is fundamentally sound value chain management practice for all organizations to employ cost-effective, standard approaches for identifying items, participants, locations, procedures and assets. For example, for hospital treatments to be speedy, certain, low cost, safe and secure, the following need to be tightly defined and identified: patients, clinicians, locations, diagnoses, treatments, medicines, equipment, suppliers and original manufacturers.

A sound data architecture must include standard messages, identities, auto identities, master data and dynamic data, and these are defined below (Section 15A.2, Reference 11).

Messages

Standard communications of orders, completed deliveries, invoices and payments, together with many other instructions or records – eg such as inventory levels, out-of-stocks, production and delivery schedules, patients to be treated, taxes due from citizens, bank account balances.

Identities

Standard descriptions and code numbers for the products and services being traded or provided. To these IDs can be added auto-IDs, which enable the automatic recognition of items by means of, for example, laser beam scanning of barcodes or the use of radio frequency identification tags (RFID). The best-known ID system for frequently used items is the Global Standards 1 System (GS1 – **www.gs1.org**). The worldwide banking system uses the SWIFT standards – **www.swift.org**. The engineering world uses the STEP standards – **www.steptools.com**. Unfortunately, too many organizations employ ad hoc and/or outmoded systems.

Master Data

Describes in a detailed, systematic manner:

1 the participants in a value chain;

2 the items and services they trade;

3 the locations used;

4 the procedures they follow and the activities they undertake;

5 the assets they use in the procedures.

Master data should be held in structured, rigorously managed (electronic) files, which are accessible under secure conditions by all relevant participants in the value chain:

- Participants are customers; suppliers; individuals (eg citizens, patients, employees); agents (eg banks, insurance companies, transporters); and authorities (eg government departments, police, Customs, health and safety bodies). Such master data define each participant in terms of name and description, locations (code, address) and role.

- Items are goods and services. Such master data define each item in terms of name and description, ID item codes, key characteristics, category (classification); and also, within rigorously related files, specific prices and costs and, next, detailed designs and technical specifications.

- Procedures are conversions, from one state or stage to the next, of items (eg rules for processing materials, construction/assembly, recipes for cooking foodstuffs); or of participants (eg treatments for patients or procedures for managing citizen services). Such master data describe what would be done by whom under specified circumstances.

- Assets are the unchanged equipment or facilities used in procedures (eg rolling mills for steel or X-ray machines for patients). Such master data define each asset in terms of description, asset code, location, usage.

A simple order (see Figure 8.4) only involves participants and items using agreed standard codes to represent each.

Customer A is defined by a code applied to the particular trading location (from which an order is issued or to which a delivery is to be made (Location Code NNNN1)). The customer instructs the supplier via a communication to an agreed supplier location code (Location Code NNNN2) to deliver 10 cases of Item X and 5 cases of Item Y to Location NNNN3 on DD/MM/YY.

FIGURE 8.4 The simple order

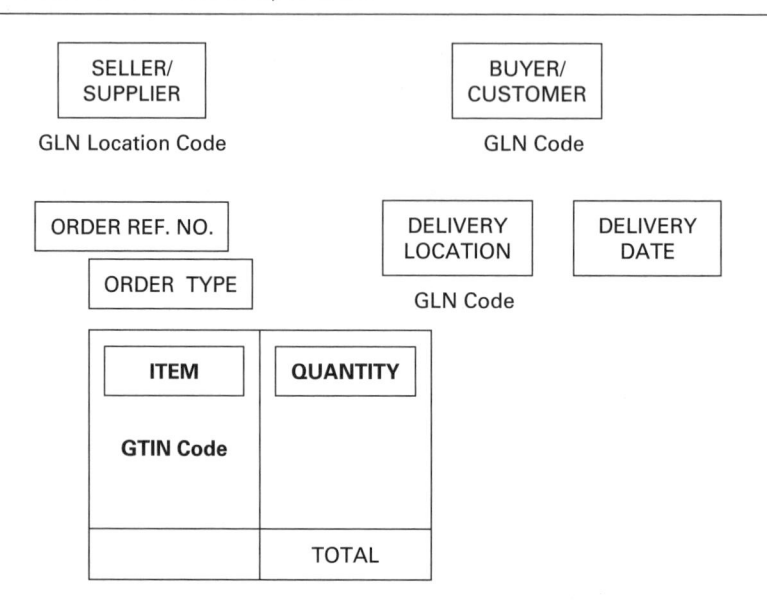

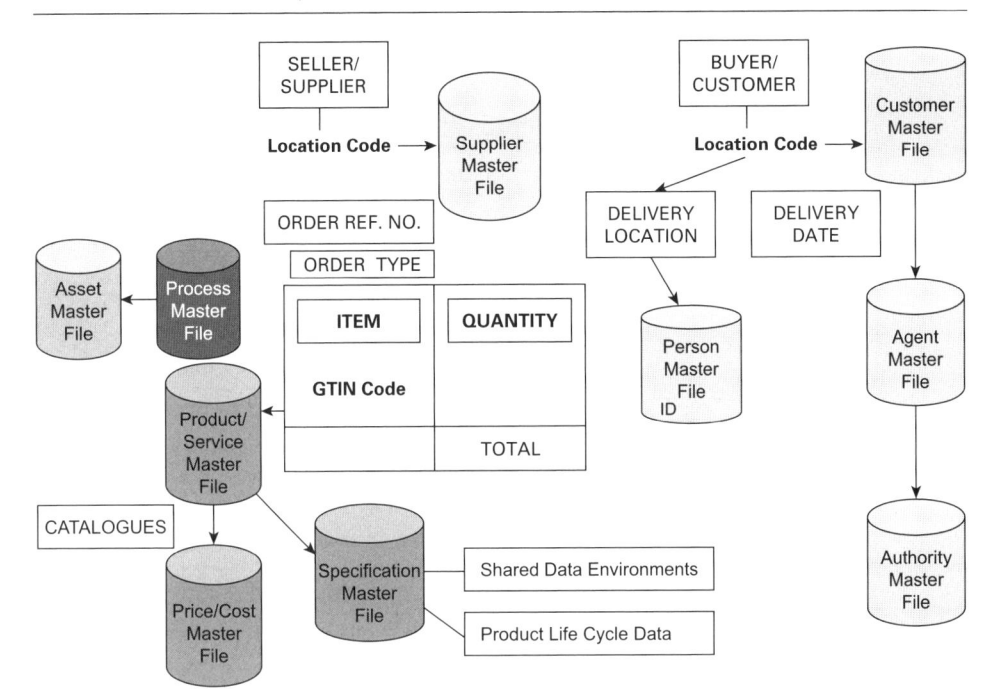

FIGURE 8.5 Simple e-business: the complex order

A complex order (see Figure 8.5) could involve, for example, a customer (a GP or consultant) ordering a supplier (hospital radiologist) to process an individual (patient) on CAT machine type 3 by date DD/MM/YY. See Figure 8.6 for an outline usage of health value chain data.

(Figures 8.4 and 8.5 follow the Simple.e.business rules (Section 15A.2, Reference 12 and in **www.unece.org/CEFACT**.)

Master data need to be structured by all value chain participants in an agreed standard way. They must also be pre-aligned or synchronized among the participants before exchanging orders and other electronic messages. This is similar to having a published catalogue defining items and prices. Ideally, most of the data in a master data file should be created as early as is practicable in the value chain, for example by the original manufacturer. Master data require to be time-stamped to indicate within which dates they are applicable. Master data are therefore 'semi-static' and need to be distinguished from dynamic data, which relate to transactions, events and outcomes. All master data are defined by unique, preferably meaningless, identity codes (eg Global Trade Identity Numbers – GTIN from GS1). Such

FIGURE 8.6 Health value chain master data: sources of information

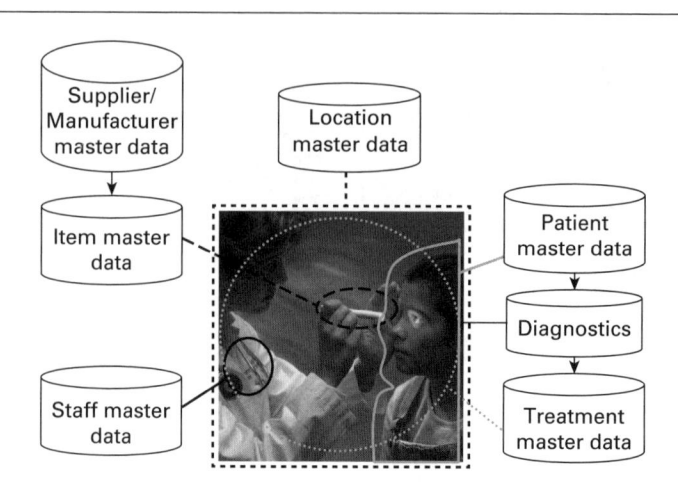

identities allow precise referencing and cross-referencing to both master data and to dynamic data files from transactions and also plans. Messages need only contain codes and quantities, and other related master data can be accessed from the appropriate file. Not only do messages become simpler, but they are all less error prone since the master data files can be rigorously policed.

Identities can then be used to support the cost-effective management and control of physical value chains via scannable symbols and RFID tags (auto-identification and data capture – AIDC technologies). This not only improves automation and potentially reduces costs, but it also enhances safety and security. For example, patients, healthcare staff and drugs can be auto-identified to ensure that the correct dosage of the correct drug is administered by the authorized professional to the correct patient via immediate links to accurate master data files. Dynamic data files can then record activities and outcomes – see Figure 8.6.

Dynamic data define the quantified objectives in the form of:

1 planned outcomes (intended volumes of activity, budgets, KPIs);

2 actual outcomes;

3 and thereby performance levels, per participant, organization, item, location, asset, activity/procedure.

Single window

In an 'ideal' world, an individual or an organization would only need to be identified once in order for all relevant parties to know with whom they are transacting business. For example, if a business is being incorporated, it should be able to answer, in one location, one comprehensive set of questions and thereby satisfy all government departments and authorities. When a business presents all relevant data to all relevant authorities via a single point of interface, this is known as a 'single window' system. Similarly, if a business has defined to the Customs authorities which products it wishes to import and export, from which suppliers and customers in which countries, these data should be immediately available to all relevant authorities so that the business can be promptly informed of all relevant legislative and administrative requirements and options. Having satisfied all formal requirements once, a recognized business's goods and services should then be able to flow without hindrance, provided there are no significant changes to the above elements.

Clearly, personal and financial data require strict security controls; but the single-window principles and benefits are the same as those outlined above: define objectives, supporting processes and value chains, master and dynamic data, together with related AIDC systems.

Financial flows

One of the simplest and most standard orders is a banknote: 'I promise to pay the bearer on demand'. Financial flows often only define the accounts of the payer and the payee and which banks are being instructed to make and receive the payment. It is beneficial if payments can also be related to the delivery of a specified product or service by a supplier; for example, an invoice which can be cross-referred to the delivery of a product or service; a stage payment on a contract after specified work has been completed ('earned value'); a payment to or from the government as a result of fulfilling certain criteria. The successful management of most organizations depends on being able to relate the actual to the predicted (planned) flow of funds, and to be able to explain variances. It is therefore vital that the finance and banking industry, which is truly global in scope, becomes fully involved in the development of comprehensive and cost-effective value chain standards.

Recommendations

 a Subject to further analysis and development, the plan to payment process described above should be adopted as a global standard within which all component proposals for related value chain standards are evaluated. No sub-optimal, partial standard which conflicts with the above should be imposed on industries and countries by a government body, agency or other organization. This does not deny the right of any firm or organization to state its business requirements to its trading partners and to seek agreement on a cost-effective joint solution. Nevertheless, its attention should be drawn to the above solution.

 b No electronic business standard should be imposed which is based on a single technology or communications protocol. Standards must be based on agreed cross-industry, cross-country standard business process and data architectures. Technologies continually evolve and change – fundamental process and data architectures based on the above principles will stand the test of time.

 c Work should continue to refine related value chain management standards, aligning with the best standards already in place or currently evolving, eg those endorsed by the Memorandum of Understanding between ISO, ITU, IEC and UN-ECE/CEFACT.

 d Do not proceed with designing or implementing a computer system until appropriate process and data architectures have been well defined and agreed with those who must employ them.

Value chain process analysis and driving business change

In any process-mapping initiative, understanding a value chain will require considerable input from all the parties involved in the process. Value chains are inherently more complex than an internal business process, since there are multiple stakeholders from many organizations. There is, however, a shared objective of providing a cost-effective product or service to customers. And that is why so many organizations are now interested in process and performance improvement related to their value chains.

The traditional approach

A traditional approach to process mapping typically involves a 'brown paper' exercise, requiring key individuals involved in the process to be available, usually in a large meeting room, so that the existing processes can be drawn together. This produces a significant risk due to the use of an unstructured approach.

Gaining 'buy-in' to the proposed changes could be difficult to achieve because the usual means of communication to individuals within an organization are via presentations, written documents or diagrams placed on the shared file system. Inherently, these materials can be insufficiently connected to the analysis side of the process.

This method of communication has been a significant problem for many projects because:

- an unstructured approach lacks governance and compliance;
- agreed changes to processes need to be communicated to all parties in a structured manner, and not by ad hoc means;
- the written content created can be inadequate as a blueprint for action.

In addition, since process mapping should be looking ahead to continual process improvement (rather than a 'once-off heroic effort'), the traditional approach lacks the feedback, change control and communication capabilities needed for long-term and sustained value chain improvement. In many modern organizations, people communicate by means of a wide variety of modern technologies (phones, e-mail, Facebook, Twitter, blogs, let alone meeting and speaking, with more technologies and techniques to come). Therefore, for an organization to become and remain truly cost-effective, it must design, build and implement sound and effective process and data architectures which operate well both internally and across its value chains. Both the process designs and their communication to value chain participants must be focused and clear.

The emergence of business process analysis and mapping tools

Business process analysis (BPA) tools are available to help capture and analyse processes in a robust system-supported way. But, perhaps surprisingly, these tools have traditionally been aimed at technical staff and business process analysts, and have paid scant regard to ordinary business users who may want to engage in process capture; or indeed the end users who need to be informed of the results. Consequently, the majority of BPA tools are over-engineered for business users, and use a technical notation format better suited to system or workflow design, rather than being suited to the needs of ordinary end users.

End goal – the thought-through value chain

Because of the technical bent of many BPA tools, they tend to be used predominantly in relation to process automation. True end-to-end business processes (such as encountered in the value chain) are likely to be composed of many manual tasks as well as an increasing number of system automated tasks. So the typical utilization of BPA tools and techniques can all too easily overlook key areas of value chain improvement. In truth, both manual and automated tasks must be identified, improved and adopted by all stakeholders for sound process improvement to become a reality.

Value chain collaboration and competition

09

Introduction to competition and collaboration issues – legal and practical

Sections 9A and 9B cover the two vital and related topics of value chain competition and collaboration. We begin by looking at legal issues in 9A, and suggest practical steps for making valuable progress with value chain partners while also remaining within the law. In Section 9B we look at the practical benefits from, as well as the difficulties with, collaborating with key value chain partners in various contexts. Achieving a viable, sustainable and mutually beneficial balance between competition and collaboration is one of the fundamental business issues, and this demands ongoing intelligent management. Remember that value chains greatly benefit when standards of identification, processes, data and communication are common to the partners. When these are in place, all value chains can perform better and participants can focus on developing their competitive edges – value chain managers cooperate, value chains compete.

9A Staying within the law

Legal issues

1 Risk of anti-competitive behaviour proscribed by UK Competition Act 1998, UK Enterprise Act 2002 and Articles

101 and 102 of the Treaty on the Functioning of the European Union (TFEU)

- Does the collaboration:
  - have an *appreciable effect in a relevant market* in the EU/UK by preventing, restricting or distorting competition (where markets are defined by way of the 'SSNIP' or Small but Significant Non-transitory Increase in Price test – the smallest geographical area in which a hypothetical monopolist could profitably sustain a price increase above competitive levels)?
  - result in the undertakings abusing a dominant position in the market?
  - produce an agreement not to sell to a competitor's customers, or refusing to supply?
  - result in 'unfair' prices to customers or suppliers?
  - tie the purchase of goods or services to the purchase of other goods or services?
  - involve directly or indirectly fixing prices; sharing markets or sources of supply; limiting or controlling production volumes in order to drive up prices; manipulating markets; controlling technical development or investment (all are restricted activities regardless of whether the effect on the relevant market is appreciable or not)?
- If the answer to any of the above is 'Yes', participants are potentially in breach of competition law, which has sanctions including:
  - disqualification as a director;
  - criminal offence for individuals dishonestly engaging in cartel agreements that have a price fixing effect, which may result in imprisonment and unlimited fines;
  - financial penalties up to 10 per cent of worldwide company turnover;
  - third-party claims for damages against those found to have behaved in an anti-competitive manner

2 How to comply with competition law.
- cooperate with non-competitors[1] OR
- Cooperate with competitor companies where the participants to the cooperation cannot independently carry out the project or activity covered by the cooperation[2] OR
- Cooperate where the cooperation concerns an activity which does not influence the relevant parameters of competition[3] OR
- Show that cooperation results in economic benefits, adds value generally (eg improvements in the production or distribution of products or the promotion of technical or economic progress) and that such benefits favour not only the parties but also consumers[4] (although if there are less restrictive ways to achieve benefits, if claimed efficiency gains do not justify anti-competitiveness, and if parties are dominant, no elimination of competitors is justified) OR
- Show that cooperation results in environmental benefits, eg reducing companies' carbon footprints, pollution; although the reduction must be quantifiable. If arrangements are purely a screen for anti-competitive practices, competition rules apply.
- In relation to pricing:
    - Make sales or output information sufficiently historic and aggregated such that it is impossible to identify individual undertakings' competitive behaviour.
    - Employ no concerted practices restricting prices in broadest terms.
- Information exchanges:
    - These must not reduce/remove uncertainties inherent in a competitive market. This applies more to competitors than to customers and suppliers.
    - Acceptable to share, for example, statistics concerned with total market volumes over time in specific industry sectors. Conduct limited benchmarking exercises. In case

of collaboration aimed at optimizing net added value for customers, data that measure success can be shared (eg retail in stock per cent; inventory and forecast accuracy in sales and order forecasts), and also data that measure exceptions.

- Avoid:
  - restrictions on advertising;
  - making joint purchasing/selling arrangements;
  - insisting on codes of conduct that place limitations on competition or exclude parties from sharing benefits not otherwise available;
  - any insistence that collaborating members use standard sets of terms and conditions;
  - provisions restricting non-competing retail parties from fulfilling unsolicited sales (ie passive selling).

Practical issues

3 Develop a sound collaborative framework agreement (CFA). A well-drafted framework agreement for collaboration is trust and relationship based – lighter on detail than a contract for outsourced services, and more a code of conduct. However, specific provisions should be considered for:

- planned goals and objectives of participation (this assists in evidencing compliance with competition law);
- making any up-front investment by a single party recoverable before benefits are shared;
- procedure for participants (including mentors and process leaders?) to share management;
- new joiners and leavers (eg confidentiality, and step-out processes);
- defining liabilities of partners and limits on mutual responsibility (participation is 'own account'; no authority to bind);

- clear lines of communication and reporting;
- ownership and licensing provisions for all participants of any intellectual property rights used or created during collaboration (co-ownership not usually prudent – better to have perpetual transferable licence to use technology);
- conflict resolution (an alternative dispute resolution process adjudicated between the parties should be built into the agreement as a first forum, spun out to independent alternative dispute resolution (ADR) supervised by the Centre for Effective Dispute Resolution in the event matters remained unresolved). Recourse to the courts is less desirable. Framework agreements should be governed by the laws of a convenient jurisdiction.

4 Communication
- Need to:
  - identify planned goals for the participants;
  - identify unifying factor for collaboration:
    - participants in collaboration to measure the costs and performance of activities, resources and the objects that consume them in order to generate more accurate and meaningful information (activity-based costing or activity-based management techniques) and share conclusions of data to identify unifying factor or synergy ripe for exploitation;
  - employ clear lines of communication and reporting of ABC data without sharing, which measures success of collaboration.

5 Timing of collaboration
- to realize maximum potential from collaboration, logistics service providers need to be involved 2–3 years before the launch of a product
- may arise out of need eg a change in laws in the Netherlands regarding the sizing of Regional Distribution Centres led to Kimberley Clark and Unilever collaborating through a shared distribution centre

- Non-logistic based collaboration. For example Proctor & Gamble using Web 2.0 to access the web to reach a pool of global experts in order to cut its R&D budget; or Kimberley Clark's collaboration with Axela Biosensors, (a Toronto based company specializing in medical diagnostics), which gave Axela access to about 150 worldwide patents and applications; Proctor & Gamble making all its 27,000 patents (of which only 10 per cent were in use by the company), available for licence on a website **yet2.com**

6 Costs
- The CFA may allow for the recovery of parties' reasonable costs of participation
- The CFA might encompass both gain-sharing by participants and up-front investment by a sponsor. Consequently the agreement could cover capital and revenue costs and provide for benefits to be shared after the investment costs are recovered by sponsor. Similarly, if up-front investment to cover capital and revenue costs is shared, then benefits should be shared equally
- A CFA might also cover benefit sharing between participants in a sub-group of a trade association, although here caution must be exercised to avoid contravening competition law
- If there is any sharing of costs, gains or benefits, then a transparent method of accounting for these needs to be provided (in such a way as to avoid too much sharing of sensitive commercial information which could contravene competition law)

9B Effective value chain collaboration and competition

Introduction

The preceding section – 9A – has outlined the issues relating to working with value chain partners within the framework of competition law. This section attempts to cover the ongoing fundamental question of how to achieve the best balance between competition and collaboration. There are no definitive nor unchanging answers. Nevertheless, neither competition nor collaboration alone will maximize individual or collective value. Therefore each organization should continually address how to achieve the best blend.

Without competition, organizations and individuals become complacent, inefficient and costly. Without collaboration opportunities for improving both demand and supply are missed. Every customer needs competition between his suppliers in order to improve costs, margins, quality and service. However uninformed competition can be wasteful where there is a lack of a common understanding among suppliers of the customer's fundamental objectives, of his key specifications and his business processes, and of where data to be shared are inaccurate or not aligned.

Care should be taken to establish the nature and degree of collaboration to be undertaken with each of competitors, customers and suppliers. For example, sharing price data with competitors is normally contrary to the law, while agreeing with all value chain partners' common standards for logistical handling units or scannable symbols is normally eminently sensible and permissible. Insight is required into the potential benefits of shared trading data, such as orders or planned production, with each type of partner. There should be a common understanding of the real size and pattern of end-user demand. The Forrester Effect (see Figure 11.2) illustrates how the failure to focus on the end user and to share relevant and timely data leads to growing costly deviations from optimality by all value chain participants. While sharing certain financial data may well be anti-competitive, sharing inventory data may be counter-productive if all customers increase their orders to maximize their shares of limited stock availability. However, sharing end-user demand or consumption information along with relevant volume plans may be essential in order to integrate and optimize all value chain partner responses to fluctuating demand. This may be the only mutually cost-effective way to make profitable use of scarce production and distribution capacities, especially when a new product or service is being launched.

Particularly in large organizations, official public stances on such matters as collaboration, competition, risk sharing, encouraging small suppliers and paying to terms may in practice be observed by only a few of the many functional silos. Therefore it is vital to focus on what organizations and their components actually do rather than on what they say.

Categories of value chain relationship

Organizations vary widely in relation to the relationships they have traditionally had with value chain participants. The differences can result from particular industry customs and practices, from chief executives' styles and from global and local circumstances. Here are some of the more common categories:

1 Arm's length: Information exchange is limited to 'need to know'. Suppliers are informed of specifications to be met and not of customer objectives. Suggestions for improvement are not sought from suppliers. 'The customer knows best.' Plenty of alternative suppliers are believed to exist who can meet the 'straightforward' requirements. This approach sometimes occurs in small to medium scale manufacturing and in parts of the public sector.

2 Confrontational: This approach is aggressive, price-focused and unstable. Contractual arrangements are rare. There may be retrospective demands for discounts, or delayed payment of bills – 'Partnershaft'. Quality and service are demanded rather than jointly developed. The reward mechanisms for customer staff focus on achieving high revenues and margins in the near term, especially within the commercial functional silos. Logistics staff may preach or even employ collaboration, but buyers are confrontational. This approach is not uncommon in retailing.

3 Aggregate and sequential: Best prices are believed to result from aggregating demand to the highest level in relation to both spend and to the number of items and product/service categories. There is limited understanding of service sustainability and through-life costs, and it is believed that risks can and will be transferred to suppliers via 'tight' contracts. Invitations to tender are issued which are too static, and a 'beauty parade' of suppliers is conducted. The lowest

prices bid are usually accepted. Customer understanding is limited in relation to who are the best-of-breed suppliers in each market, and why. Often procurement or commissioning consultants are employed who have little more real awareness than the customer. Prime suppliers may be appointed in order to avoid the customer doing the hard work of effectively defining objectives, markets, projects and value chain relationships. This approach is too common in the public sector.

4   Oligopolistic/oligopsonistic: A few large customers facing a few large suppliers. Some value chain management management data may be shared; but with great circumspection, and often via trade associations.

5   High-tech: Where complex long-lasting products are involved, much technical data needs to be shared with suppliers both for development and support. This involves high security and accuracy requirements for reasons of both safety and commercial value – eg aerospace and defence.

6   Creative and dynamic: Sharing overall objectives and underlying approaches in order to ascertain what is really needed and what development paths are likely to be most beneficial to both parties –'This is what we do with what we buy, and this is what our customers and end users really require in order to perform well.' This is 'dynamic acquisition', which encourages the supplier and the customer to work together in order to produce joint creative solutions. This involves an ongoing cost-effective balancing of supply and demand at levels of risk which are understood and accepted by the key stakeholders. There is transparency of sub-contracting. The required capabilities of both customer and supplier teams are understood and fulfilled on an ongoing basis.

7   Integrated: In some situations it may be necessary to have a sole supplier whose operations are fully integrated with those of the customer in order to achieve a necessary high standard of quality, service, safety and security – eg glass container supplies into a food factory, and polyethylene terephthalate (PET) bottle-blowing units in a soft drinks factory.

8 Dysfunctional – What seemed like a good idea at the time does not work in practice – cf. 'The Law of Unintended Consequences'. The price may be good but the total cost and service are poor. Circumstances may change and unforeseen substantial risks appear. This occurs too often with outsourced supply chains which are poorly defined and managed. There is a failure to understand what processes, data, capabilities and performance measures are required to manage a value chain which is not under direct control, and which may be severely affected by external forces, such as global political and economic factors.

A process for effective collaboration

The following steps are proposed in order to achieve the best balance between collaboration and competition in developing and operating a modern value chain.

a Evaluate how competition law applies.

b Analyse the relevant markets, their 'rules', the best suppliers and how they do business, along with trends and dynamics.

c Define relevant, consistent objectives with value chain partners and understand potential areas of conflict.

d Define what can wisely be included within contracts, what needs to be framed within a creative and dynamic relationship and what should be left to market forces.

e Agree and implement the key business processes and procedures internally and externally. Examine these in relation to R&D, projects, event and change management and ongoing operations. Keep these as simple and as standard as is practicable. Agree process role models (see Chapter 8) as to which people in which functions are to reach specific decisions based on defined data and timescales. The particular approaches to be adopted will vary to some degree from industry to industry, according to the degree of technology involved, and also according to the social anthropology of the various 'tribes' and their customs.

f Define and implement the data architecture required to manage the value chain both internally and with partners. These will include structured messages, standard identities, auto-identities, data elements, master data, and dynamic data, data synchronization or alignment, and measures of control and performance, both financial and operational.

g Define and implement staff capabilities, training, continuity and reward/discipline mechanisms appropriate to the value chain and its partners.

h Review achievements and amend accordingly.

Notes

1 Source: Guidelines on the applicability of Art 81 of the EC Treaty
2 Ibid.
3 Ibid.
4 Art 81(3) Treaty of Rome

Effective and integrated value chain planning
'Failing to plan is planning to fail'

10

Summary

All business plans should clearly define where net value is to be added across an organization's internal and external activities and processes – its value chain. Also, we must show how this value chain is to be improved by enhancing utility and benefits, revenue and profitability, performance and service, while reducing total costs. Each plan must also describe the relevant uncertainties, that is, both the exploitation of opportunities and the mitigation of risks. Plans must cover the physical/quantitative aspects, the financial measures, the informational/ data contexts, and of course the human/cultural and organizational factors. The detailed, integrated internal plans to which people are going to work in practice are of much greater importance than any glossy, externally published summary plan, no matter how inspiring the strategic prose. Beware of photographs of smiling people tastefully arranged by the public relations department. Good, rigorous, painstaking, sometimes annoying planners are worth their weight in gold.

Dynamic planning

Business planning is a dynamic process. There can be plans relating to shifts, days, weeks, months and years, with different horizons. An agreed systematic procedure is essential for updating plans and budgets, in relation to past performance and to changing future expectations.

In particular, business plans should cover:

1 The particular value and utility which the organization aims to provide to the end user or consumer.
2 Revenue streams – under various market scenarios.
3 Market competition, and thereby market shares. Undertake market research. Also try to define the alternative, potential providers who could alter the market. Define some contingency plans.
4 For non-profit organizations, turnover/total value of services/throughput/financial surpluses/output/benefits/outcomes for individuals and groups.
5 Costs – under the various market scenarios:
   a capital and operating ;
   b average and marginal;
   c through-life costs;
      i including internal and external dependencies;
      ii and including any disposal costs at end of life;
   d other charges, including local, national and international taxation.
6 Profits and cash flows.
7 Funding – how much, when, from whom, at what costs. Include any securities required by lenders.
8 Particular resources and prerequisites – required facilities and infrastructure.
9 People – numbers, capabilities, training and development needs, environment and culture.

10 Product and technology development and R&D, relating to end products, to ingredients/components and also to facilities and systems. R&D should also aim to reduce the key uncertainties across the value chain – notably to open up new opportunities, but also to mitigate risks.

11 Marketing and sales, including intermediate customer service. These also cover macro-marketing to all key stakeholders and to those who can have a major impact on the business, as well as micro-marketing aimed at immediate customers and consumers.

12 Supply markets and procurement (acquisition/commissioning). Buying is almost as important as marketing and selling – perhaps less 'style' but often more 'substance'.

13 Asset utilization – load factors and capacity analyses. Too little and/or too much capacity. Strike an effective balance between being 'lean' and being 'agile'.

14 Business process and value chain developments (including collaboration and competition factors) with customers and suppliers, and also with end users, competitors, prime and sub-contractors and stakeholders. These initiatives will focus on identifying, analysing and strengthening the weak links in the value chain.

15 Key change projects, including major investments and IT.

16 Capital investment. Planned return on capital employed (ROCE).

17 Information, data and accounting.

18 Safety and security.

19 Environment.

20 Legislative and political matters, at home and abroad.

21 Governance – must not be neglected.

Too many business plans lack rigour, integration and commitment. A sound plan must show the following:

1 The business objectives which the plan supports. These will relate to performance (eg outcomes, output, throughput,

quality, service); to cost; and to time; and will encompass the trade-offs within and between these. The critical success factors and KPIs must be defined in a balanced manner.

2 Key actions – what needs to be done, shown in relevant detail.

3 Responsibilities – who is to do each action and what are the relevant accountabilities. This must include a comprehensive view across the relevant value chains – both internal and external responsibilities. Confirmation that resources are capable, available and committed for the required time periods.

4 Benefits and costs.

5 Timescales – by when each action is to be completed.

6 Prerequisites and dependencies.

7 Uncertainties, both opportunities (positive) and risks (negative) – what if various events occur – consequent impacts and probabilities; risk ownership and mitigating actions – these need to be fed into the plan, and not managed separately.

8 A sound mechanism for measuring progress against the plan, and for reporting deviations. If these are agreed to be significant, there may need to be prompt re-planning, and this requires an agreed, systematic framework.

Integrated business planning

Clearly, there is a strong relationship between planning, forecasting and estimating. These latter two activities are important and must be integrated with the plan (Figure 10.1). The following matters, however, need to be borne in mind:

1 Sound forecasts and estimates depend on sound diagnoses, and all depend on reliable data. At the end of 2014, *The Sunday Times* published an analysis of the relative success of well-known economic forecasting organizations using their scale of 1 to 10, in relation to the following factors – GDP growth;

inflation; current account balance; unemployment; bank rate. The best result was 8 out of 10 by Capital Economics and the worst was 0 out of 10. From a total of 39 forecasters, 12 scored 4 points (including the Economist Intelligence Unit) and 12 scored 3 points (including the Office of Budget Responsibility and the European Commission). These results indicate that economic forecasting is difficult and few bodies do it well. Therefore, although you need to take account of other bodies' forecasts, ensure you have an integrated planning system which enables you to deal well with inaccurate forecasts.

2 Mathematical models can be instructive and greatly aid diagnosis. They are less good at prognosis or forecasting. This is because the economic (and physical, astrophysical, biological, environmental, social) world is much more complex than can be described and predicted purely in mathematical terms. For example, in econometrics, models with four or more independent variables face increasing difficulties in explaining and predicting the dependent variable because of the increased number of interactions among the independent variables, let alone the difficulties of then estimating future values for the independent variables (or forecasting weather, or human behaviour). Too many leaders of organizations have a limited grasp of mathematics. Worse, they can be afraid to say that they do not understand the mathematical models they have been asked to endorse. They should say that they will not agree to proceed until they are given a satisfactory explanation.

3 Computers are able to calculate faster, but not necessarily better. They can be very instructive in quickly exploring alternative scenarios, in doing sound sums and in examining the effects of different levels of uncertainty. Computers cannot be better than the data entered and the human assumptions made. Remember GIGO (Garbage In Garbage Out). Sound human judgement remains essential.

FIGURE 10.1   Integrated business planning

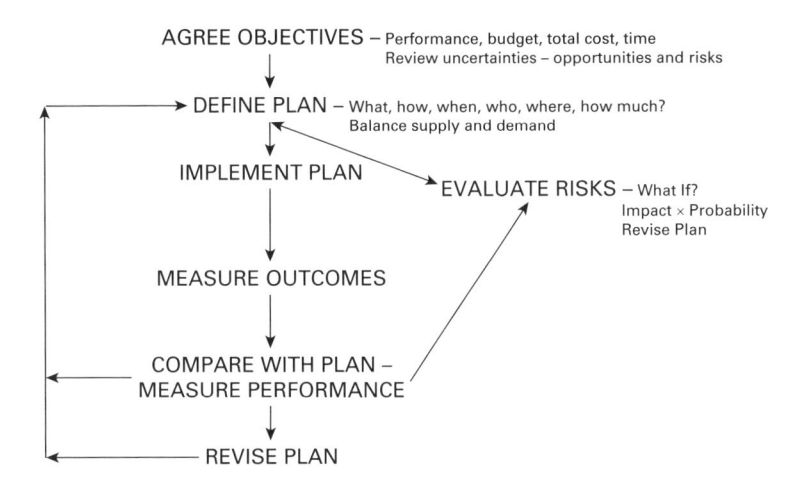

```
          AGREE OBJECTIVES – Performance, budget, total cost, time
                    │         Review uncertainties – opportunities and risks
                    ▼
          DEFINE PLAN – What, how, when, who, where, how much?
                    │    Balance supply and demand
                    ▼
          IMPLEMENT PLAN ───────────▶ EVALUATE RISKS – What If?
                    │                                  Impact × Probability
                    ▼                                  Revise Plan
          MEASURE OUTCOMES
                    │
                    ▼
          COMPARE WITH PLAN –
          MEASURE PERFORMANCE
                    │
                    ▼
          REVISE PLAN
```

As described in Chapter 9, legitimate and constructive collaboration can be better at reducing uncertainty than merely relying on statistical forecasts.

> I keep eight honest value chain men,
> They taught me all I knew
> Their names are What and Why and When,
> And How and Where and Who;
> Ably supported by How Much and What If.

With apologies to Rudyard Kipling.

Managing uncertainty

11

The consequences of not identifying and managing uncertainty, opportunity and risk cost effectively, and how to do better

Introduction

This chapter discusses the critical importance of analysing uncertainty, and its components opportunity and risk, across your value chain, especially when you are undertaking a major initiative or project. In particular, you must define, own and manage your risks as well as your opportunities. No one else can do this for you. Uncertainty, opportunity and risk are not sufficiently well understood, be it in financial markets, in computer systems, in complex projects, or even in auditing, economics and business studies. The cost of this confusion can be seen in financial turmoil, failed projects and initiatives, excessive costs and disappointing benefits, and in unreliable value chains.

Key academic disciplines (mathematics, science, engineering, medicine, economics, psychology, philosophy, finance and management) too often define uncertainty, opportunity and risk differently, not only between but often within the various branches of each discipline. Furthermore, the definitions are often made in ways that confuse the non-academic reader and thereby lead to poor decision-taking.

Too many decisions are taken without a careful analysis of the related uncertainties, or without distinguishing risks from opportunities. Some individuals are happy to take particular decisions so long as the opportunities appear to outweigh the risks by a good margin, and especially if it is someone else's money they are risking.

To most people who take decisions, uncertainty means being unsure of what is going to happen. It is also being unsure of what decision then to take and of the likely outcome. Uncertainty consists of two components – the opportunity to benefit (a positive) and the risk of loss (a negative), allied to how an individual or organization values these in relative terms.

Too many people believe that contracts can be written which 'transfer risk' (and management responsibility) from the customer to the supplier. In reality, for risks to be mitigated effectively they must be defined, understood, owned and managed by the customer. The supplier can only agree to accept defined and limited material, financial and legal consequences if specific risks materialize. The supplier can always walk away (eg by refusing to proceed, by going bankrupt, by demanding more money) from a contract, and the customer is then left bereft of their objectives if they have not otherwise been able to mitigate their risks. Even an insurance policy only 'assigns' certain financial consequences to the insurance company, while it is you who are dead, injured or without your home, prized possessions or business. Therefore you must always try to define and understand your risks as well as your opportunities, and to own and manage them effectively.

The consequences of failing to understand uncertainty and to define, own and manage risks can be seen in many arenas. Thus, financial markets develop ever more sophisticated portfolios and computer models which regularly serve to deceive the unwary who do not fully understand the risks lurking within the sophistication. Seemingly intelligent people agree to invest in technology, and notably in computer hardware and software, without demanding explanations they really understand, and without balancing risks with opportunities. Time and again, many complex and costly public and private projects substantially fail to meet their objectives (which themselves too often lack clarity) because the risks have not been well defined nor mitigated.

The consequences of failing to analyse and manage uncertainties, and of attempting to transfer ill-defined risks which cannot and should not be transferred, can be seen in the failure to deliver cost-effective results, or even any worthwhile results, from some key projects. These include certain UK government-inspired Private Finance Initiative and Public–Private Partnership projects, and also Family Credits, Farm Payments, and NHS Connecting for Health. This last involved negotiating very tight regional contracts with a number of suppliers, all intended to be completed at the same time. Some suppliers ran into technical problems, some into project management problems and others into escalating costs. Certain suppliers therefore failed to deliver adequate results or decided not to complete their projects.

The wiser course of action would have been to be much clearer about the most important deliverables, about the balance between opportunities and risks, and about corresponding benefits and costs. This would enable the definition and testing of solutions and the mitigation of risks on a small scale (this process is known as evolutionary prototyping – a fundamental technique). It is also a fundamental prerequisite to gain the prior commitment of key stakeholders (such as doctors and hospitals) to common and cost-effective process and data architectures and to integrated plans.

Although risk analyses are now usually mandatory for most major investments and decisions, such analyses are often inadequate and misinterpreted, with the result that many projects are undertaken in a 'conspiracy' of optimism with eventual disappointing results. This chapter and the next provide an overview of the key contexts in which the management of uncertainty, opportunity and risk is essential – for ongoing operations of organizations and their value chains, for major change projects, for personal and physical safety and security, for financial portfolios and for research and development.

This chapter redefines more simply and usefully what is meant by uncertainty and its two constituents, opportunity and risk. The chapter and the next also propose new rigorous frameworks within which demand (objectives) and then supply (means) are specifically analysed, and then balanced dynamically (dynamic management of projects and initiatives) in the context of the related uncertainties. Decisions are then taken in the light of the key stakeholders understanding and accepting the risks as well as the opportunities, along with their planned mitigation. I indicate how data to support decision-taking and ongoing effective management should be structured and employed within collaborative value chain management.

Definitions

Life as we know it is irredeemably uncertain. We do not know for certain what is going to happen. Furthermore, we either do not know what the options for action are, or what each action implies (we lack dependable data and/or the means to analyse it effectively). Even after further research, we can be unsure of what then to do. A decision is not only influenced by an objective analysis of the uncertainties, but also by our subjective attitude to these. Once a course of action has been decided, we too often remain unclear on the outcome.

Uncertainty arises from forces and events which are more or less difficult to predict, and from their interactions with human perceptions and behaviour. Uncertainty relates to situations where the outcome cannot be predicted accurately. The outcome may in varying degrees be good (there are opportunities) or bad (there are risks). All key desired objectives and outcomes can and should be expressed as precisely as is practicable, and in terms not only of potential benefits and costs, but also of a range of impacts and probabilities of occurrence. For example, a desired outcome and its corresponding plan of achievement may be expressed as a 10 per cent probability of gaining £1,000 or a 50 per cent probability of losing £100. Or, suppose I need 98 per cent certainty of having a new job by 1 January, with an 80 per cent probability of the salary being in excess of £50,000. While I may accept with some equanimity the risk of losing £100, I need the near certainty of a new job in order to avoid the risk of losing my house. That is, there are distributions of impacts and related probabilities which need to be defined and understood. These distributions are rarely 'bell-shaped', with equal probabilities of gaining or losing, although several estimating systems unwisely assume this. For example, 'three-point estimating' most often assumes a symmetrical distribution on either side of the 50 per cent 'most likely' estimate –

10 per cent (0.1 probability that results will be better than this level) and 90 per cent (0.9 probability that results will not be worse than this level). In complex situations there are usually more risks than opportunities, and the degree of potential loss is often substantially greater than the potential gain – see Figure 11.1.

FIGURE 11.1 Distribution of risks

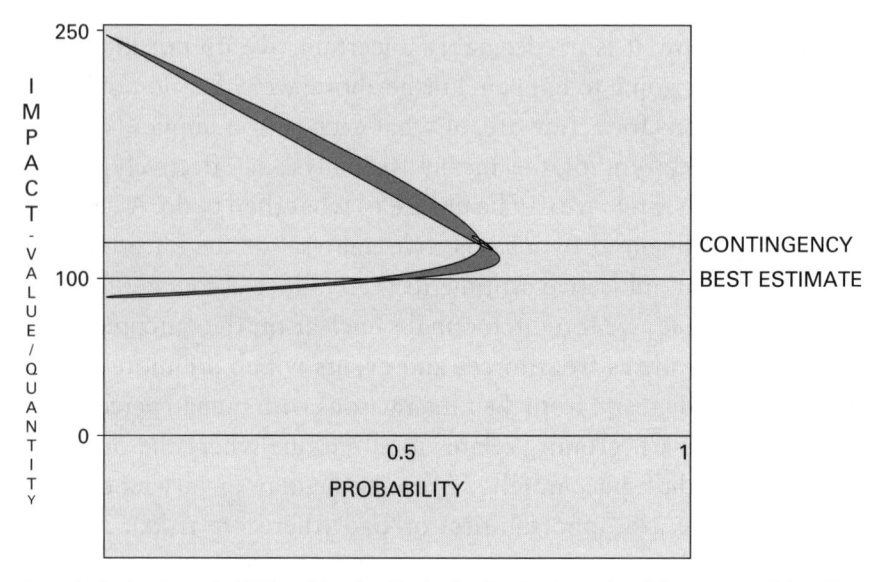

Curve indicates the probabilities of beating the best estimates for cost and time are much less than those of exceeding them. For performance the reverse would be true. The contingency allows a limited excess before new authorization is needed.

Wherever practicable, estimates of potential impacts and probabilities should be made, preferably quantified, but certainly specified. There is no excuse for not grappling with uncertainty, however wearisome the exercise, and this chapter and the next provide a discipline to follow.

Opportunity is a situation which has potential for the realization of net value through the investment of skill, money and resources. The outcome is uncertain and there may be several ways to realize an opportunity. These need to be evaluated along with the risks of loss. Nevertheless, a potential course of action is 'opportune' when there is a conjunction of desired objectives with what are believed to be available resources, realistic timescales and a favourable 'climate'.

(Compare the Latin word *opportunus* describing a favourable wind that blows towards a safe harbour).

Risk is an event with a severity of impact and a probability of occurrence that could have a significant *adverse* effect on the achievement of objectives. Risk always denotes a potential negative impact. However, a belief that risk can be positive often leads to management failing to define and manage it rigorously. In real life, when a doctor offers a patient a treatment he or she should say: 'This treatment does not have a certain, guaranteed outcome. It gives you the opportunity of leading an active life, but it has the following risks.' The doctor does not say: 'There is a risk that you will recover.'

Following a review of many economics, business, government and financial documents, it is evident that there is no consensus on the meanings of uncertainty, opportunity and risk, and much confusion. For example, the UK Treasury Orange Book, which defines how government projects or public investments should be justified (now enhanced by a bigger Green Book), maintains that risk can be positive or negative, and that it can (should?) be transferred to suppliers. It is therefore hardly surprising that the costs of large, unanticipated and poorly managed risks continue to hit the taxpayer hard; and worse, end users suffer from the failures.

In a situation of low uncertainty, investing money in a business or a project will usually earn a low rate of interest. There is little in the way of potential profit, above the rate of interest, as a recompense for taking the risk of losing one's investment. *Interest* is a payment for parting with money for an agreed period of time, and its rate is affected by demand and supply factors, along with specific and general risks. *Profit* is the return from exposing one's resources (land, labour and capital) to uncertainty in the belief that the opportunities exceed the risks. High risks usually demand high potential rates of return in the form of interest, capital gains and/or trading profits. The degree of uncertainty is most often a function of the size and complexity of the situation and the timescale within which the objectives need to be achieved. If I am substantially uncertain and I am also averse to risk, I demand a higher internal rate of return from a project, and this in turn discounts to a greater degree future net benefits (profits) in favour of early returns.

Uncertainty explored

Uncertainty arises from two main sources. The first source is the 'natural' states of the physical world, its peoples, its markets, its current and potential products and their many varied and complex interactions. Uncertainty can be generated by poorly structured objectives. Too often these are merely sub-optimal and unbalanced 'targets'. Predictions of outcomes can and should be made, especially by using relevant and timely data. Planning is vital – failing to plan rigorously, and integrating risk mitigation with opportunity exploitation, is planning to fail, expensively. But, uncertainty reigns. Diagnosis of past events is often more accurate than prognosis of what could occur, and forecasts are unlikely to be more accurate than the assumptions on which they are based.

The second source of uncertainty is self-inflicted, by the failure of people and organizations who are participants in a particular value chain to share timely data and to cooperate effectively. If we are wise, we learn to live better with the first source and to minimize the second through effective joint management of each value chain. We need to ensure that the value chain tiers do not become a vale of tears. To the degree that we are unsure of what another person or organization is going to do, we either live with poor service or we cover (assure) ourselves by employing additional resources, just in case. 'Uncertainty is the mother of inventory', and of production and distribution excess capacities, of waste, write-offs and other costs. The distinction between these two sources of uncertainty is neatly encapsulated in the Value Chain Management Prayer: 'Give us the will and the insight to remove uncertainty caused by lack of cooperation and communication, the character to accept irreducible uncertainty caused by dynamic users and markets, and the wisdom to know the difference.'

The uncertainty resulting from the divergent reactions of each successive participant in a value chain to actions (and data) by their customer was first identified by Jay Forrester in 1961 in his book on *Industrial Dynamics* – see Figure 11.2.

Even where end-user demand is relatively stable, each internal and then external function back along the value chain will have its own reasons for imposing increasingly large fluctuations in what it transports

FIGURE 11.2   Forrester Effect

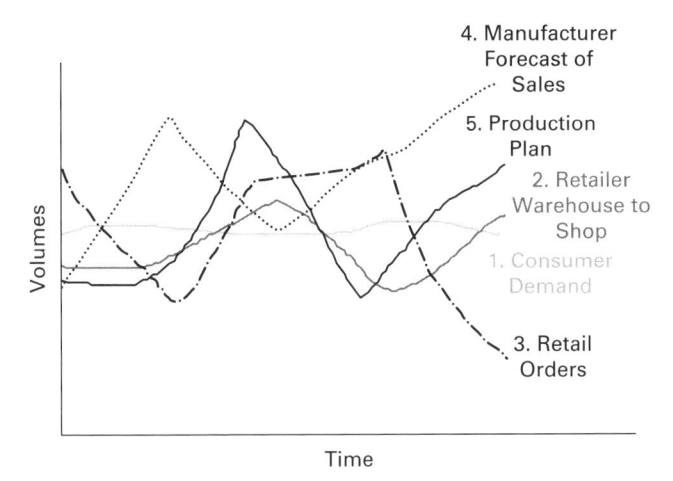

Even if demand is steady, each part of the value chain can add its own uncertainties.

or produces, in order to meet the demand of its own immediate customer. This supply chain 'silo effect' has been further elucidated by many analysts across various industries (eg Gillian Tett (2015) *The Silo Effect*, Simon and Schuster, New York). However, the conclusions and actions resulting from such analyses have not always been sufficiently beneficial. Often, businesses have been inspired simply to improve their statistical forecasting or to share a variety of unfocused data. Personal experience leads to the conclusion that all key value chain participants need a shared view of the levels of ongoing end-user usage or demand, along with agreed publication of relevant plans and other data.

For example, in the 1970s, electronic point of sale scanning (EPOS) was introduced in order to make pricing more accurate and service more speedy within supermarkets. When food manufacturers enquired of the supermarket owners about access to these data in order to improve their understanding of consumer responses, they were told that they could have weekly data in arrears at a significant charge, on the grounds that the data seemed to be mainly of value for marketing purposes. The food manufacturers therefore gleaned data from each stage in the value chain – point of sale, warehouse movements, retail head office orders, manufacturer sales forecasts and production plans. With colleagues, I used this information to prove to the retailers that the free daily provision by them of EPOS data within 24 hours, together with an agreed sharing of sales and delivery plans, would improve consumer service and sales at a lower total joint cost. By doing this, food manufacturers and retailers could thereby increase the size of the total revenue cake by reducing uncertainty, and thereafter argue about how to cut the cake between them.

Further reductions in uncertainty can therefore be achieved by developing a role model (see Chapter 8), which indicates which business function in each value chain participant needs to communicate which data, to whom, on a structured timescale (from product concept to final sell-through). In the late 1990s, an internet system (NIMBUS) was developed which allowed such structured joint decision-taking and planning to be undertaken in a shared computer environment. This further linked each value chain partner's internal decision-taking structures and communication systems and helped to minimize the risk of mis-communication and error.

A fundamental factor in minimizing value chain fluctuations that arise from the failure to cooperate and communicate is therefore to have a joint picture of what the end user of the product or service is consuming, allied with an agreed joint decision-taking process, and supported by shared plans and data for each key intermediate stage in the value chain, for example delivery plans and production plans. It is sometimes less wise to share inventory data, since customers, and even one's own sales force, tend to respond to low but viable stock levels by over-ordering in order to protect their individual positions, thus precipitating unnecessary out–of-stocks. Consequently, one of the component factors in reducing uncertainty is enhanced trust in one's customers and suppliers (and also one's employees).

The decision to share information with a customer or supplier always needs to be taken in such a way as to enhance cost-effectiveness and not to damage competition – see Chapter 9. As noted earlier, Adam Smith remarked in *The Wealth of Nations* that 'People of the same trade seldom meet together even for merriment and diversion but the conversation ends in a conspiracy against the public, or in some contrivance to raise prices.' Nevertheless, much uncertainty and associated costs can only be reduced by systematic collaboration among value chain participants – when value chain managers cooperate well and wisely, value chains compete better.

Uncertainty and lack of understanding

Many risks come to fruition because individuals have not asked enough of the right questions at an early stage, and have not been adequately aware of what they were buying. Many examples could be given of such mistaken products and services – it would be unkind to speak ill of the dead, for example Open Systems Interconnection (OSI), NHS Connecting for Health.

Does this happen because too many people, including those in top jobs, are unwilling to say 'I do not understand this, and I am not going to proceed until I do'? Or is it because they have in fact delegated decisions with huge potential implications and risks away from themselves? Or again, is it because the lustre of short-term opportunities for gain blinds those with pay packages that incentivize the short term despite the longer-term risks facing shareholders, employees and customers?

Thus, many financial crises have been, and continue to be, caused by organizations undertaking financial transactions over which they had no effective governance. Complex options, derivatives and packages of sub-prime (ie very risky) loans have been bought by people and institutions who should have known better. Too many organizations have allowed traders to make inadequately assessed and controlled transactions which had the potential to bankrupt the business – see Chapter 6, Section 6A.1 on the finance value chain.

A similar situation holds with companies and governments undertaking investments in computer systems they clearly did not understand. Too often they appear to be at the mercy of technologists and consultants.

If you understand only the opportunities in a proposal and not its risks, do not do it.

Attitudes to uncertainty, opportunity and risk

In all areas of life we decide whether action is required, and what that action should be, by reference to the importance or impact of the outcome to us in relation to the costs of achievement. What degree of certainty or probability do we aim for? Having selected a course of action, we then should define the risks to the achievement of that outcome (objective) so that these may be mitigated to a level that we understand and accept. The degree of mitigation will depend on our *risk attitude* and on the *cost–benefit relationships* involved.

Many people maintain that they are *risk averse* – they wish to minimize the maximum that can go wrong. It is often the case that such people may be *risk ignorant* rather than risk averse. For example, it is just not wise to be risk ignorant in defence, since military expenditure has to focus on agreed areas of risk. Similarly, we should not be risk averse since we incur major risks in order to avoid the *ultimate risks* of defeat, death and destruction. One must be very *risk aware*.

At the other end of the spectrum are those who indulge in *opportunity admiration* or, worse, *risk addiction*. These may be individuals for whom a project with a largely certain outcome holds little attraction. For these people the challenge is to overcome the risks and to seize the opportunities. Their dangers lie in not specifying the risks well, and in not ensuring that their partners and customers own and manage the risks with them. A useful matrix for analysing attitudes to uncertainty, opportunity and risk is shown in Table 11.1.

TABLE 11.1 Attitudes to uncertainty, opportunity and risk

	attitude		
	uncertainty	opportunity	risk
awareness	essential	essential	essential
analysis	essential	essential	essential
ignorance	dangerous	foolish	dangerous
admiration	foolish	valuable	dangerous
addiction	foolish	exhausting	dangerous
aversion	limiting	foolish	limiting

Integrated planning and risk methodology

The methodology is as follows. The sequence is very important (see also Chapter 4):

1 Define objectives clearly, and the degrees of certainty required. Avoid introducing unbalanced sub-optimal targets, which often become subject to the Law of Unintended Consequences. Objectives relate to a combination of performance, contract cost, through-life cost and time. Define the uncertainties that surround each of these, while also selecting the specific opportunities to be exploited.

2 Define the ultimate risks. Are there overriding adverse outcomes that must be minimized?

3 Define the research and development programme that will support the better exploitation of the opportunities and the better mitigation of the risks.

4 Define the business processes and the value chain by which the objectives will be achieved. It is unwise to focus only on the key suppliers and customers with whom one has contracts. All key participants in the value chain who could significantly affect outcomes must be identified and their roles established. The process architecture must be supported by an effective data architecture so that accurate and timely control may be achieved.

5 Define and implement any organizational changes only after the process architecture is agreed. Furthermore, organizational cultures are as least as important as structures.

6 Define the plan to achieve the objectives – what, how, when, by whom, what cost, what interdependencies (eg of other projects and programmes) and what critical paths? Separately define demand (objectives) and supply (means), and then define how the two are to be kept in an ongoing cost-effective balance. Agree measures of achievement.

7 Define the expected categories of risk. Categorization aids the process of ensuring that all key areas of risk are covered, and

in a balanced way. Categories must be relevant to the operation or project in hand, and not generic categories – eg demand risks in specific markets or from competitors, specific supplier risks, technology risks, legislative risks. Within each category, define the specific risks to the achievement of the plan – what if each occurs? Quantify or specify potential impacts and probabilities of occurrence of each defined risk. Impacts are the key factors to be defined. Quantify impacts where practicable and/or describe them in relevant detail so that the mitigation becomes evident.

8 Agree risk owners and gain their full commitment – Risks *cannot* be transferred to suppliers. Risks should *not* be transferred to customers without their formal agreement or understanding. Ensure that both risk and opportunity management are fully integrated within operations and project management, and not separately managed.

9 Define how risks are to be mitigated – specify actions with benefits and costs, timescales, responsibilities and intended outcomes. Build the mitigation plan into the main plan so that there is full integration of all that needs to be done. Some texts describe mitigation as comprising treating, or terminating or tolerating. Detailing a specific action with costs and benefits is much better.

10 Measure achievement against plan, and where necessary redefine plan and risks.

11 Ensure that there is an effective system of governance covering all the above. Too often, once opportunities have been defined and a plan agreed for achieving these, appropriate governance is not put in place. Measures and controls must be appropriate to the nature of what is being undertaken and to its risks. For example, management consultants extolled the virtues of empowering staff to exploit opportunities in Enron in the US energy markets, and elsewhere, without adequate governance and risk management first being put in place. As a result, control was lost, with disastrous consequences.

There are a number of approaches to business and project planning and control, with varying degrees of complexity and administrative overhead. None guarantees success, although all have their merits. In general, it is clear that current approaches to project definition, planning and management leave substantial room for improvement. Some of the main problems facing business and project planners are:

1. A plethora of requirements, hurdles and gateways from outside authorities, reviewers and 'scrutineers' which must be surmounted for further work to be authorized. As a consequence, managers may come to see progress as satisfying the outsiders rather than meeting the real objectives. This approach could be characterized as the 'British Leyland School' of trying to 'inspect in' quality, as opposed to incorporating it from the start. If quality is not inbuilt, not only will there be additional costs of inspection but there will also be subsequent customer complaints and faults to repair. Thereby came the demise of British Leyland (and other companies). Published rules must be practicable for reasonably capable managers to assimilate and to put into effect – there should be only a moderate number of understandable, integrated and rigorously enforced requirements for defining and managing a project or operation. Speed, certainty and cost of achievement are often in inverse proportion to the number and complexity of the hurdles to be cleared.

2. Lack of effective access to relevant and timely data. Too often management accounting and control data are inadequate, particularly in the public sector and in certain financial arenas. Financial accounting to support top-level reporting often takes precedence over the information needed by the managers who are actually supervising the operations or the project. One of the scarcer and more valuable skills is the combination of sound understanding of a business allied to the ability to collect and structure data to support its dynamic operation at all key levels.

3. Lack of capable and experienced staff – with adequate continuity in post – in both the customer and the supplier. Far too often, people are appointed to key project roles in order to 'give them broader experience' prior to taking up a senior

appointment at a relatively early date. Those appointed to teams must be capable of piercing uncertainty, of managing the identified opportunities and risks and of spotting others as they appear, as an integral part of delivering the required project outcomes. Appointments to key complex projects should ideally be made for the duration of the project (or of key components), and must comprise the specific capabilities required. Do not have institutionalized incapability.

4 Inadequate definition of demand and supply and rigorous procedures for bringing these into balance. While customers and suppliers rarely have identical objectives, processes and systems, these must be consistent. The proposed solution is detailed in the next chapter on dynamic management of projects and initiatives.

Risk lists and matrices

It is vitally important for all stakeholders to be aware of all the principal risks and the associated impacts and probabilities. It is dangerous for the key stakeholders only to see the top five or ten risks and only to view the matrices that show the results of multiplying impact times probability. For example, if an organization or a project has 50 major risks, it is highly dangerous to focus only on the top 10. At one point, the UK Home Office was cited by the Cabinet Office as employing 'best practice' through whittling down the risks to be considered by its management board to just the top five!

Furthermore, stakeholders need to know if there is a 3 per cent risk of losing £100 million, or a 40 per cent chance of losing £10 million, since the former may bankrupt the business or project – even though the latter has a net potential value of £4 million (0.4 times £10m) compared with £3 million (0.03 times £100m). That is, the key focus must be on impact, since mitigation has to relate to its effect on the organization.

Risk lists are often inadequate to a significant degree in terms of focusing the attention of both the project team and its higher authorities on real risks and on prioritized, cost-effective actions.

Risk matrices show the results of multiplying impact by probability; eg an impact of 2 out of 3 multiplied by a probability of it occurring estimated at 1 out of 3, ie 2 × 1 = 2. Matrices can be used to focus management on what are calculated to be the most important risks (3 × 3 = 9). Such matrices are common, but should be used sparingly, if at all, since they can easily mislead management – potential impact is more important than probability of occurrence (ie 3 × 1 is more important than 1 × 3). In addition to 3×3 matrices, there are others such as High, Medium, Low, or Red, Yellow, Green. Others are 5 by 5 – a spurious increase in accuracy. For example, parts of the NHS use the following for severity of incident (impact): catastrophic, serious, moderate, minor and negligible. Why include a negligible (ie no meaningful value) risk? Impacts are considered in relation to injury/illness, patient experience, effects on systems, projects, targets and objectives, complaints/claims, financial loss and adverse publicity. The NHS describes probabilities as: almost certain, likely, possible, unlikely and rare. On a 5 × 5 matrix, a rare catastrophe is a 5 (1 times 5), as is an almost certain event of negligible consequences (5 times 1). In practice, these need very different approaches to management, since the consequence of loss is far more important than the chance of loss; that is, the rare catastrophe is the risk that demands special focus.

Too often, completing such matrices is assigned to separate 'risk managers', whose analyses are cursorily reviewed by senior management, and thereafter the required mitigation is incomplete and unintegrated with business and project plans.

There is a real danger of the assessment and management of risk and uncertainty being done in an insufficiently rigorous and integrated manner – through ticking boxes, filling matrices and submitting reports to an unresponsive hierarchy. Do not fall into this trap.

Notes

1 Forrester, J (1961) *Industrial Dynamics*, Pegasus Communications, Waltham, MA
2 Tett, G (2013) *The Silo Effect*, Simon & Schuster, New York

Dynamic management of projects and initiatives

12

A structured framework for managing complex projects, initiatives, investments and value chain operations.

The approach proposed in this chapter includes a mechanism to ensure that projects, initiatives, investments and value chain operations are defined and analysed systematically, consistently and rigorously before full permission to proceed is agreed (and thereafter as major changes occur). It also requires that, wherever appropriate, one integrated and synthesized approach replaces the plethora of current requirements. Doing this ensures that managers and their stakeholders can follow a single, coherent approach which can then be taught, assimilated, applied and enforced with the maximum likelihood of success. Given life's uncertainties, there can be no guarantees.

In order to describe clearly how dynamic management of projects and initiatives (DMPI) works, the main focus will be on the definition and management of complex projects. Nevertheless, this approach also works well in analysing and managing most situations of substantial uncertainty and risk.

DMPI requires the rigorous definition of both demand (objectives, outcomes, ends) and supply (means), and also their ongoing cost-effective balancing, at levels of uncertainty and risk which are understood and accepted by all key stakeholders of a project. It seeks to replace static, aggregate and sequential procurement. This too often falls into the trap of inadequately defining demand or capability requirements first, at too high a degree of aggregation and of risk. Then one searches for a single supplier (rather than seeking the best suppliers for each key component of the project), who appears to be prepared to accept ownership of the risks within the available funds, or at least to sign a contract which superficially implies this commitment. DMPI probes the nature of the uncertainties surrounding complex projects. It also demands that project teams operate within a framework of sound governance and risk management, as opposed to empowering project teams to do their own thing in the vain hope that the opportunities will far outweigh the risks.

DMPI demands that project definition and planning, operational planning and business planning are conducted in an integrated manner. Actions to mitigate risks or to exploit opportunities must be integrated (resourced and prioritized) within these plans – see Chapter 10.

Methodology

Complex projects, initiatives, investments and value chain operations have four related objectives, each of which needs to be clearly defined:

1 *Performance*:
   a capability – outcomes, output, throughput – in relation to intensity and diversity of use;
   b quality – reliability, meantime to failure;
   c safety – ability to use without danger to operatives and others;
   d security – systems need to be in place to ensure that there can be no deliberate or inadvertent intrusions.

Performance can also be defined in relation to the number of items of equipment, eg five small tankers might be capable of delivering as much as one supertanker, while also providing more security, at a lower developmental risk, but at an anticipated higher total cost.

2 *Contract cost*: capital and revenue costs incurred to provide the equipment, facilities and systems to deliver the performance, normally defined in contracts with suppliers and in internal budgets. It is vital to distinguish the overhead costs of undertaking the project from the average costs of each deliverable, and from the marginal costs of additional units.

3 *Through-life cost*: costs to use, maintain, support and enhance the facilities and systems throughout the working life, and then to dispose of what is no longer needed. This includes the cost of providing and/or enhancing all the support facilities, costs of recruitment and training and costs of meeting legislative or societal requirements.

4 *Timeliness*: delivering performance and incurring cost when planned. The time to reach agreed decisions also needs to be factored in.

These objectives define the demand of the customer. Each aspect of demand has related requirements for certainty, as well as related risks. However, demand has inadequate meaning unless there are effective means of supply. Each aspect of supply also has associated uncertainty and risks. Both demand and supply must then be brought into balance by means of trade-offs which systematically reduce the levels of uncertainty and risk while exploiting opportunities wisely.

Trade-offs need to be made within each of these objectives, and then between each. For example, there will be a trade-off between speed, range and payload (performance factors) for a plane, ship or vehicle, and also between these and contract cost, and through-life cost and time. Furthermore, each objective needs to have an agreed best estimate of the intended optimal value after supply and demand have been brought into balance. Two other estimates should normally

FIGURE 12.1 Managing trade-offs

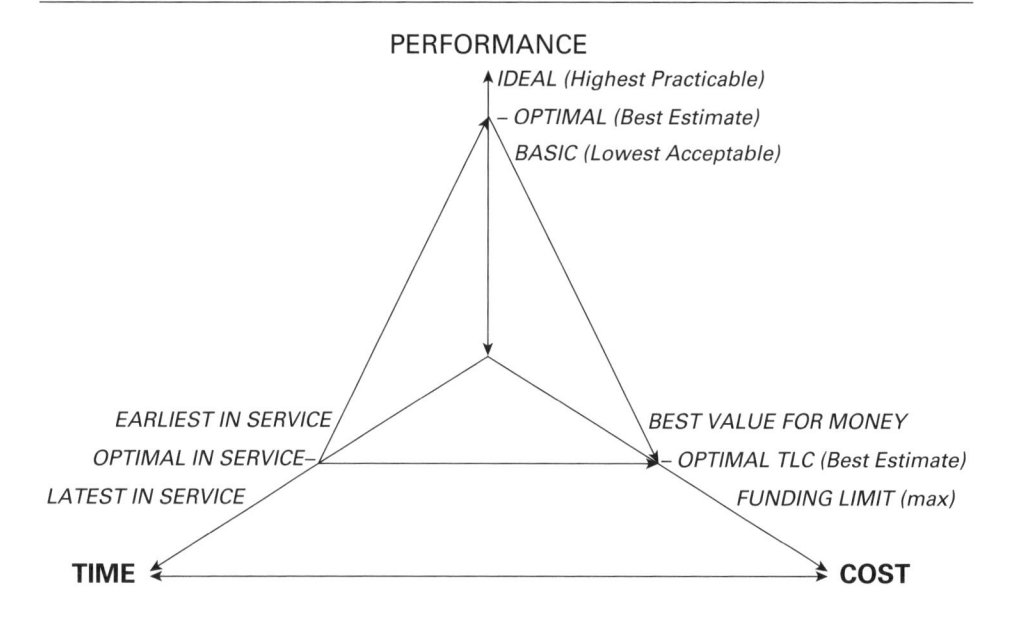

```
                    PERFORMANCE
                    ↑ IDEAL (Highest Practicable)
                    – OPTIMAL (Best Estimate)
                    BASIC (Lowest Acceptable)


    EARLIEST IN SERVICE              BEST VALUE FOR MONEY
    OPTIMAL IN SERVICE –              – OPTIMAL TLC (Best Estimate)
    LATEST IN SERVICE                 FUNDING LIMIT (max)
TIME ←                                                    → COST
```

be made for each factor – the ideal (or highest practicable) and the basic (or lowest acceptable) – see Figure 12.1.

Note that these are not the same as the conventional three-point estimates (see the section on definitions in the previous chapter) which give values at 10 per cent, 50 per cent and 90 per cent probability. In theory, 10 per cent and 90 per cent values indicate only a 10 per cent chance of being better or worse, respectively; but it is extraordinarily difficult to provide a meaningful value for each. Such 10 per cent and 90 per cent estimates do not relate to the expected probability of occurrence of each value in practical conjunction with the values of the other relevant factors. So, for example, performance may be the most important factor, requiring a 95 per cent probability of achievement, while time may have more flexibility with only a related 75 per cent probability requirement not to exceed a certain date. Furthermore, the best estimate should have a much better than 50 per cent probability of achievement after risk mitigation. Otherwise more mitigation is needed.

Each key estimate needs a specific defined probability of achievement along with the key associated risks and their predicted impacts.

The risks of failing to achieve the best estimate almost always exceed the opportunities to improve on it; that is, there is not normally a bell-shaped distribution of impacts and probabilities around the best estimate, but one that is skewed towards the risk of being worse, and often much worse. Opportunities to do better tend to be limited, and often require additional resources – see Figure 11.1. Note that a contingency also needs to be defined. This shows the level by which a key estimate can be exceeded (in the case of cost and time – or not met in the case of performance) before formal permission is required from relevant stakeholders. This type of diagram needs to be prepared for all key estimates and the associated risks mitigated until a 'satisfactory shape' is agreed.

A common example of the danger of not associating risk with estimates relates to international projects. The predicted savings related to sharing development costs with overseas partners, and thereby to reductions in average unit costs, need to be balanced carefully against the wider uncertainties and risks deriving from the complexities of collaborating with more, and more diverse, customers and suppliers. These include time and cost factors involved in reaching agreement on more complex specifications and in developing and managing multinational value chains.

The main differences between existing approaches to project and operations management and DMPI is that each objective is to be specifically defined in relation to both the demand from the customer and the supply capability, on an ongoing basis; and also the associated uncertainties and risks; along with the degree of imbalance between supply and demand. To the extent that uncertainties and risks are not well defined, quantified, owned and managed in relation to both supply and demand, at every key stage of a project, there must be a formal rebalancing exercise to redefine an ongoing cost-effective relationship between supply and demand at levels of uncertainty and risk which are understood and accepted by all key stakeholders. Dependencies also need to be identified in relation to other projects, programmes and related resources and capabilities.

Figure 12.2 illustrates the matrix to be used to provide each estimate.

FIGURE 12.2 Dynamic project and uncertainty management matrix for defining and managing complex projects

	PERFORMANCE	CONTRACT COST	THROUGH LIFE COST	TIME	
Desired degrees of certainty	IDEAL highest				Trade-offs within objectives
	OPTIMAL best estimate				dependencies
	BASIC lowest acceptable				Risks and mitigation

TRADE-OFFS AMONG OBJECTIVES

Demand (supply) and supply (means) are separately defined and then dynamically balanced, by means of trade-offs within and between each of performance, contract cost, through-life cost and time. Uncertainties – opportunities and risks – are specified, along with dependencies. Risks are mitigated to understood and accepted levels. (Worked examples follow.)

Figures 12.3A, 12.3B and 12.3C provide numerical examples.

The demand matrix is created first – what degrees of certainty are needed in relation to each of the objectives? What are perceived to be each of the key risks and their impacts and probabilities? What are the key dependencies with other projects and programmes? Where demand is insufficiently clear and stable, and where the associated risks are too great, demand is adjusted via trade-offs: similarly with supply. Many of the key factors which must be considered, along with the most likely risks, should be summarized in a checklist to ensure that a rigorous approach is adopted. The composite balance matrix, found in Figure 12.3C, is then completed; it defines the best estimates relating to an agreed balance between supply and demand. A risk register can then be prepared, which ranks all risks by magnitude and category – providing risk definition, impact, probability, ownership and mitigating actions, costs and expected value after mitigation. The risk registers of all key stakeholders should be substantially similar and certainly consistent, although not necessarily identical.

All the above needs to be done thoroughly before effective project and business planning, or even staffing, can be completed. Otherwise there is the real danger of having a 'great' plan for a poorly defined, resourced and/or inadequately de-risked project. Risk mitigation must be built into the plan.

FIGURE 12.3A Dynamic acquisition – demand example

	Performance (probability)	Contract cost (probability)	Through life cost (probability)	Time (probability)	Dependencies	Risks
IDEAL	80 mph – 500 mls 45 tonnes **0.60** 60 mph – 600 mls 45 tonnes	TOTAL COST £55m **0.85**	TOTAL COST – £750m **0.90**	2012 **0.50**		Distributions of key risks Max impact
OPTIMAL	70 mph – 500 mls 40 tonnes **0.80** 50 mph – 600 mls 40 tonnes	Development – £20m Average cost – £100k Marginal cost – £60k **0.90** TOTAL COST – £50m	Running costs – £400m Maintenance – £100m Upgrades – £150m New facilities – £45m **0.85** TOTAL COST – £700m	2012 **0.80**	Total and max Loads to be carried. Other workloads on facilities	– on contract £15m with probability of 0.2 – on TLC £100m with probability of 0.3 RISKS incl funding, unclear exisiting TLC, overseas demand.
BASIC	65 mph – 500 mls 40 tonnes **0.98** 45 mph – 600 mls 40 tonnes	TOTAL COST £45m **0.95**	TOTAL COST – £750m **0.97**	2010 **0.99**		

DYNAMIC ACQUISITION PROJECT Z – 1. DEMAND
HYPOTHETICAL EXAMPLE – Truck 500 units, 20 year life

FIGURE 12.3B Dynamic acquisition – supply example

	Performance (Probability)	Contract Cost (Probability)	Through Life Cost (Probability)	Time (Probability)	Dependencies	Risks
IDEAL	65 mph – 500 mls 35 tonnes 50 mph – 600 mls 40 tonnes **0.80**	TOTAL COST £42m **0.90**	TOTAL COST - £850m **0.80**	2011 **0.90**		
OPTIMAL	60 mph – 500 mls 35 tonnes 50 mph – 600 mls 35 tonnes **0.90**	Development - £10m Average Cost - £80k Marginal cost - £60k **0.95** TOTAL COST £40m	TOTAL COST - £800m **0.85**	2010 **0.95**	Best supplier will need substantial additional business to justify our contract costs/prices. This is likely, but timing is key.	Risks Distribution - Max Impact -£8m on Contract: Probability of 0.1 -£30m on TLC: Probability of 0.15 RISKS incl Best supplier has high order book. Latest tech. is immature. Domestic supplier needs the order
BASIC	50 mph – 600 mls 30 tonnes **0.95**	TOTAL COST £35m **0.98**	TOTAL COST - £900m **0.98**	2009 **0.99**		

DYNAMIC ACQUISITION PROJECT Z – 2. SUPPLY
HYPOTHETICAL EXAMPLE – Truck 500 units, 20 year life

FIGURE 12.3C Dynamic acquisition – balance example

	Performance (Probability)	Contract Cost (Probability)	Through Life Cost (Probability)	Time (Probability)	Dependencies	Risks
IDEAL	70 mph – 500 mls 40 tonnes 50 mph – 600 mls 40 tonnes **0.85**	TOTAL COST £48m **0.85**	TOTAL COST - £700m **0.90**	2012 **0.80**		
OPTIMAL	65 mph – 500 mls 40 tonnes 50 mph – 600 mls 40 tonnes **0.90**	Development - £15m Average Cost - £90k Marginal cost - £60k **0.90** TOTAL COST £45m	Running Costs - £410m Maintenance - £95m Upgrades - £140m New Facilities - £45m **0.85** TOTAL COST - £690m	2012 **0.80**	Role of lead supplier for through life support. Release of land etc, for new maintenance facilities.	Risks Distribution & Risk Register – Max Impact - £10m on Contract with Probability of 0.10 - £50m on TLC with Pr. of 0.15 RISKS include R&D funding & timing Late supply would impact vital ops.
BASIC	65 mph – 500 mls 40 tonnes 50 mph – 600 mls 40 tonnes **0.95**	TOTAL COST £42m **0.92**	TOTAL COST - £680m **0.80**	2011 **0.95**		

DYNAMIC ACQUISITION PROJECT Z – 3. BALANCE
HYPOTHETICAL EXAMPLE – Truck 500 units, 20 year life

Application to financial investment and to value chain operations management

This approach to defining and balancing demand and supply is equally valid when applied to considering organizational or governmental initiatives, financial investment and to managing ongoing value chain operations.

A government's or organization's initiatives should define clear and cost-effective outcomes for the end beneficiaries, and be much more than 'headline grabbing'. What is the core purpose of each initiative?

An investor looks for:

1 Performance – returns in terms of growth of income and/or capital, together with investment safety and liquidity.

2 Timescales – the internal rate of return of the investor is used to define a payback period over which the defined performance should be achieved.

3 Cost – the investment outlay along with related management costs. Consideration also needs to be given to the opportunity cost of capital (what the money could have safely earned elsewhere).

The investor must consider not only his or her demand for these outcomes, and the trade-offs within and between them, but also what the various financial markets are willing and able to supply, the uncertainties surrounding demand and supply, and then how to balance supply and demand dynamically, while mitigating risks to an agreed level.

Similarly, an ongoing value chain operation must try to deliver:

1 Performance – service, throughput and output levels, capacity utilization, quality and consistency. Safety and security are also vital.

2 Timeliness – just on time. This can also include flexibility of response to changes in demand.

3 Cost – capital, revenue, management and through-life costs.

Again, supply is balanced dynamically with demand via a thorough review of uncertainties, and by using systematic trade-offs to achieve acceptable outcomes, service levels and net added value at agreed levels of risk.

Conclusion

The current lack of clarity in defining objectives and uncertainty, and in distinguishing risk from opportunity, is costing us dearly: in financial markets, business and project management, in both the private and public sectors and in everyday life. Uncertainty is always with us, and risk, even when defined and mitigated, always retains the capacity to dent if not destroy the best-laid plans of mice and men. Nevertheless, we can and must do better in structuring our understanding of and response to uncertainty, opportunity and risk. DMPI offers an improved approach which should enable projects, initiatives, operations and financial managers and their senior management, along with all key stakeholders, to benefit from more certain and hence more valuable outcomes.

Valuable steps to success and future value chain R&D

13

Twelve practical steps to success

1. Think about your existing value chains, internal and external, national and global. Define their core purposes. Map your value chains. Which end users or consumers and value chain participants, and which demand and supply markets, really matter to you? What makes each function more or less well defined?

2. What values are you going to apply? Also, define what you mean by value. What key measures are you going to use? Add to your value chain map what and where net value is, or could be, added or lost.

3. Categorize, and then define and quantify, your key areas of uncertainty, opportunity and risk. What are the relevant economic, technological, political, human and social factors? Own, manage and mitigate all your significant risks.

4. Restate, clarify, simplify and quantify your objectives. What outcomes do you wish to realize? These should be meaningful and realistic, capable of achievement by the resources you will be able to deploy.

5 Review your business process and data architectures. Identify dysfunctions in your processes, both internally and externally. Define your principal value chain communications and identities, along with your master data and dynamic data. Identify those individuals who really understand how data are and should be used across your value chain.

6 Redraw your value chain maps to show how your objectives will be best realized. Refocus and reprioritize. Redevelop your processes and data, and simplify and standardize where practicable. Include the methods by which you will manage your key direct and indirect customers and suppliers. Analyse the markets that most affect you. Who are your current and potential competitors?

7 Review and restructure your organization, culture and social anthropology. Define your detailed procedures, and develop balanced key performance indicators and targets to be consistent with your processes and objectives. Ensure that all your guidelines and procedures are integrated and synthesized for ease and effectiveness of application.

8 Develop comprehensive, structured and rigorous business plans, which also comprise risk mitigation as well as opportunity exploitation.

9 Define and communicate your measures of performance across your value chains.

10 Redefine and instil comprehensive rules for maintaining effective control and governance.

11 Implement dynamic management of projects and initiatives (DMPI). Employ evolutionary prototyping to get things right on a small and low-cost scale first.

12 Identify and develop the required management and staff capabilities and training for sound value chain management. Align these with other necessary capabilities relevant to your organization.

Proposed areas for value chain research and development

1. Rethink what we mean by values in government, in business, in the voluntary sector and in everyday life. How should these values be put into meaningful practice?

2. How should we define, measure and map value and net value added in the public and private sectors, from the standpoint of key participants and stakeholders, and especially for the end users? How should we make the end user the true focus of the key value chains, rather than an afterthought, or the victim of silo management?

3. How do we define wise and realistic objectives and especially outcomes, and support these via lower-level balanced KPIs and targets?

4. How should we evaluate potential value chain improvements, including related business processes and data?

5. What capabilities and training are most valuable to a good value chain manager? What are the key hard and soft capabilities?

6. How best can we use value chain management and related methodologies and techniques to achieve substantially more cost-effective outcomes, allied to safety and security – in the public sector, in the financial world, in health, in energy, in project management, in IT and e-enablement, in customer service and in control and governance? What are the other priority areas? What are the other most valuable methodologies and techniques for each area?

7. How to develop an agreed structured system for doing calculations rigorously and accurately? This would avoid superficially impressive mathematics and employ fresh added value arithmetic (AVA). This would become a required competence for all key roles.

8. How to simplify matters (eg objectives, processes, procedures, rules, legislation) rather than progressively complicating

everything? How do we integrate and synthesize the directives churned out by every 'official' silo in order that those who have to achieve the objectives can effectively take on board and apply all that is expected of them?

9. How do we develop far more understandable and effective means of communicating access to information, services, support and genuine care? This especially applies to services for older people and those unused to negotiating labyrinths and dealing with bureaucracies. Far too many documents, websites, customer service centres and automated answering services are not fit for purpose. Social media too often make access to sound information more complex and less dependable. Whose data and opinions should we trust?

10. Review the social anthropologies of the key functional, professional, political, social and national tribes. How can these be used to promote rather than stultify real progress for the end user?

11. What new, focused and cost-effective measures of performance are needed for the key value chains? How should these be applied to support competition, collaboration and their dynamic balance?

12. Undertake a major review of how uncertainty and its key components opportunity and risk are defined, analysed and managed. In particular, much risk management, as required by auditors and undertaken by management boards, needs a complete overhaul.

13. What related measures and frameworks are needed for effective control and governance in relation to all the key stakeholders? In the private sector, how can fully effective governance be provided by boards of directors, too many of whose non-executive directors are 'cronies' of the executives? In the public sector, how can fully effective governance be installed for ministers, government departments and quangos?

14. Apply DMPI to a number of complex situations in the public and private sector value chains.

15 Assess the most important value chains in relation to their susceptibility to stress and potential failure when key economic, social, political and environmental factors go beyond previous boundaries.

16 Redefine the capabilities required to deliver cost-effective and user-orientated key public and private services. Develop new agency organizations, along with supporting business processes and data, which will provide the agreed products and services. These agencies must aim to improve on current sterile nationalization versus privatization debates.

17 Design and develop new value chains for the most important services which support our lives, eg:

  a Health and care – what are the most important services which people value and need in relation to their physical and mental health and care? Illness prevention; sound diagnoses; thorough and cost-effective treatments and pharmaceuticals well related to individuals' requirements and reactions; aftercare in appropriate environments for key conditions and patient ages and conditions; clear and relevant contact points and communications; sound training and development of professional staff; focused and timely R&D; adequate and effective funding.

  b Environment – integrated analysis and management of the environments in which we operate. For example, what should be the value chain for forecasting weather and other relevant factors and their subsequent management? Well-dressed TV weather forecasters tell us of weather patterns with varying degrees of accuracy but deny involvement in the consequences. Various government departments and agencies deal with varying degrees of effectiveness with weather effects and human actions; eg the Department of the Environment, Food and Rural Affairs has a major focus on farming and food and also works on managing potential floods; the water industry takes the water it needs and manages sewage disposal but does not concern itself with what happens to the rest of the water; the Department of

Transport has little responsibility in relation to air pollution; it is unclear why the Department of Energy should also be responsible for 'climate change' since it has little control over either the possible causes or the potential consequences of changes to climate. Also, why should charges for energy be raised to pay for ever-changing energy policies and practices when these charges have the biggest relative impact on the poorest people? What should be the comprehensive environmental value chain, and how should it be managed?

  c Provision of adequate accommodation and sound nutrition for all citizens. What are the minimum sound standards for food and housing which should be available to all? Which groups will be adequately provided for by various market mechanisms and what public and voluntary value chains will support the rest well?

18 Research how to reform our democracy so that it is inclusively effective and it also serves as a valuable model to follow.

19 Consider how we might develop an institution that researches, redefines and teaches the totality of value and value chain management. Each of the main existing institutions focuses on a particular aspect – eg transport and logistics, procurement and supply, operations management, supply chains. Understandably, there is a worldwide demand for particular recognized qualifications which will enhance both competencies and promotional prospects. Now is the time to take a comprehensive and integrated forward step across the total value chain.

Practical exercises in value chain management

14

Exercise 1

Select two value chains – one you know well such as your college, sports club, leisure centre – the other somewhat more remote, which directly affects your life, such as a favourite shop, theatre, team you support, local government:

1 Define their core purpose, and their specific objectives – the outcomes they are (should be) trying to achieve. Who are their end users?

2 What values do they actually apply in comparison with what they should employ?

3 What capabilities do they need in their employees and management?

4 Map these value chains – end users through to key suppliers, agents, funders, regulators.

5 What are the key business processes? What are the essential data?

6 What are the marketplaces that are of most importance? How well do they function? What role does competition play and how effective is it?

7 Consider the key uncertainties. Define the opportunities for improvement. How best should they be realized? Detail the

risks faced by the value chains and their participants. Assess the risk impacts and the probabilities of occurrence. How should the risks be mitigated? (Review Chapter 6, Section 6D.2 on the sports value chain in order to describe opportunities and risks.)

8 What can you do to improve matters and to enhance value?

Exercise 2

Select an organization where you can arrange reasonable access to its data. Describe the history of its development through to its current position. Who enabled it to add value, when and how? What values has it endeavoured to apply? What is its history of enterprise? Outline what you believe are its current and also most promising future value chains. If you were in charge, what opportunities would you be trying to exploit and what key risks would you face?

Exercise 3

Select a form (paper or online) which you have been asked to complete, and also a form which is addressed to others, for example to a business seeking planning permission or an elderly person seeking treatment or care or support. Define the objectives of the forms and assess how well they meet them – in relation both to the applicant and the recipient. How clear are the instructions and how feasible is it to complete the forms accurately? How much of the requested data are likely to be used well or at all? Design a form that adds more value and fits the bill.

Exercise 4

Pick an initiative or project that you would like to see undertaken – for example to build a new community centre, to save a particular aspect of the environment, to provide support for a group of people. Define and quantify both the benefits and the costs – for whom, for each year ahead. The benefits should be tangible wherever practicable. The costs should include capital costs, operating costs and through-life costs. Show the benefits and costs in each year ahead and thereby the net values per annum. Agree a discount factor in order to calculate the net present value (NPV). Describe why you chose this discount factor. Should your project be progressed?

Exercise 5

Select a vitally important organization which is in need of reform, for example the European Union (or the United Nations, or China). What are its core purposes?

1 To keep European nations at peace with each other.
2 To foster economic growth in such a way that wealth is generated and shared fairly.
3 To maximize free trade within the EU and cost-effective trade beyond its boundaries to maintain and develop businesses and industries.
4 To develop a strong standard currency.
5 To standardize decision-taking and legislation across the EU and to progress towards political and social union.
6 To develop a European identity and culture.
7 To be a world power and a force for good. To contribute well to solving world problems – helping refugees, improving the environment, ending wars, reducing world poverty.

Are these the core purposes of the EU, and should they be? What would you recommend? What values should guide the EU? What particular value chains need to be very well managed?

Key references

15A Value chain management references

There are certain key methodologies, tools and techniques that support the analysis and management of a value chain in order to identify how it functions and to define and develop the opportunities for improvement.

15A.1 Mapping

Mapping is done via:

a Role models – see Figures 8.1 and 8.2 – described further in Reference 9.

b Process maps – see Figure 8.3.

c Swim-lane models – which illustrate the movement of decisions and information among different functions and organizations (lanes).

d Approaches to defining the make-up of shareholder value, and for modelling required improvements, eg via the waterfall effect.

e Approaches to documenting processes, such as the Universal Modelling Methodology (UMM) and the Universal Modelling Language (UML). See **www.unece.org/CEFACT**.UN. CEFACT also oversees the Core Component Directory, which endeavours to be the standard e-data dictionary; and also the UN.EDIFACT e-business messages.

f Process analysis tools (such as NIMBUS).

A key difficulty is that many current mapping and process analysis tools may describe a value chain or process well enough, but do not satisfactorily indicate the main opportunities for improvement or optimization. Furthermore, with current tools it can be difficult to show clearly the complex issues across various dimensions, along with the current and potential interactions between different factors. Therefore, further research and development are required.

15A.2 References

1. *Demand & Supply Chain Management.* See the many publications, eg Reference 5 below.

2. Cost/benefit analysis: many publications. Summarized in *54 Techniques for Business Excellence* by Mike Wash (2007), Management Books 2000.

3. Managing change and managing people: numerous publications. See *54 Approaches to Managing Change at Work* and *54 Approaches to Organisational Healing*, both by Mike Wash (2009; Management Books 2000).

4. Value chain collaboration: see 'New Ways of Working' (2009, Global Commerce Initiative). See also good material from the Chartered Institute of Procurement and Supply at **www.cips.org**, including 'Purchasing and Supply Collaboration Between Organisations'; 'Partnering'; 'Performance Monitoring of Suppliers'.

5. Value stream analysis and value engineering: these approaches are often developed for particular industries and functions, eg automotive assembly, continuous batch food production, financial engineering. Also, some approaches focus on achieving 'leanness' in supply, production and distribution, using Japanese-type techniques, and others emphasize agility or responsiveness to demand. *Value Stream Management* by Peter Hines, Richard Lamming, Dan Jones, Paul Cousins and Nick Rich (2000, FT Prentice Hall) develops a lean approach to supply chain management. Martin Christopher emphasizes an agile approach to both exploiting market opportunities and

improving supply chain cost-effectiveness in *Logistics and Supply Chain Management* (2004, FT Prentice Hall).

6 Systems engineering applies end-to-end systematic engineering principles to the design, manufacture and through-life support of products, including the systems, computer hardware and software that enable them. Sound measurement is emphasized. See International Council for Systems Engineering, **info@incose.org**. Examples of how to measure sound progress in the more 'intangible' projects such as software development are given in *Practical Software Measurement: Objective information for decision makers* by McGarry et al. (2002, Addison-Wesley).

7 'Using value networks to boost construction performance' by David Meggitt, Christie Carre and Lilly Evans. Proceedings of the Institution of Civil Engineers, *Civil Engineering* Special Issue, **165** (2012).

8 Project analysis and control tools (eg critical path analysis, programme evaluation and review technique, PRINCE 2). *Project Management* by Harvey Maylor (3rd edn, 2003, FT Prentice Hall) provides good insights to the various approaches to project analysis and management. *Managing Successful Projects with Prince 2* (3rd edn, 2005, HMSO) is the UK Office of Government Commerce highly structured approach to project management. *Project Risk Management* by Chris Chapman and Stephen Ward (2nd edn, 2003, John Wiley) focuses particularly on the definition and management of project risk.

9 Earned value management: described in detail in *Earned Value Project Management* by Q Fleming and J Koppelman (2005, 3rd edn, Project Management Institute). There are several particular industry approaches to EVM, whose effective scope continues to evolve.

10 Improving the value of repair service systems is described in 'Estimating value in service systems' by Caswell et al. (*IBM Systems Journal*, **47** (1), 2008).

11 Value chain management data architecture. A general theory of value chain management data is developed in 'D.I.A.M.O.N.D. – how to add strength and sparkle to your value chain – a general theory of value chain management data', by Tom McGuffog (2004, UK Partners for Electronic Business).
For general data standards see **www.gs1.org** – in the UK see **www.gs1uk.org.uk**. For banking standards see **www.swift.org** – in the UK see **www.apacs.org.uk**. For engineering standards see **www.steptools.com** – in the UK see **www.ukceb.org.uk**.

12 Electronic business communications. To achieve cost-effective e-business across value chains, it is essential for this to be based on sound business process and data architectures. In turn, e-business enhances speed, certainty and, when properly done, cost, safety and security. These topics are summarized in 'B.e.e. – business enabled electronically – the future for e.business', by Tom McGuffog (2002, UKPeb). Also, Tom McGuffog contributed a chapter on 'The evolution of electronic business' for *Information Communication Technology Standardisation for E.Business: Integrating supply and demand factors*, edited by K Jakobs (2009, IGI Global).

13 Governance: this is a vast topic, and clearly in need of great improvement in many areas, notably finance and banking. See *Corporate Governance Handbook* edited by AD Chambers (2009, Tottel). Also see Andrew Chambers' excellent article: 'The board's black hole – filling their assurance vacuum: can internal audit rise to the challenge?' (2008, *Measuring Business Excellence*, **12** (1)).

14 Value chains of the future: The Global Commerce Initiative has produced three reports examining future value chain issues – '2016 – The Future Value Chain', which looks at global trends which will influence the ways in which value chains will evolve; '2016 – The Future Supply Chain', which examines the influences on the physical movement of goods as the environment becomes a bigger issue for this part of the value chain; and 'New Ways of Working Together', which reviews changes in people and organizations which will be required in order to enhance the culture within a value chain. These reports can be downloaded from **www.gci-net.org**.

15A.3 Other references

a Supply chain optimization: eg SCOR (**www.supply-chain.org**). SCOR have a framework for evaluating and comparing supply chain activities and performance. They also have tools for process mapping. See also Global Supply Chain Forum, Supply Chain Guru, Supply Chain Council and so on.

b International Trade Procedures are reviewed and improved internationally via UN CEFACT (**www.unece.org/cefact**).

c Competitive advantage across the value chain: eg *Competitive Advantage: Creating and sustaining superior performance* by M Porter (1985).

d The balanced scorecard: eg 'The balanced scorecard: measures that drive performance' by R Kaplan and D Norton, *Harvard Business Review* 70 (1), 1992, pp 71–79, and numerous derivatives.

e Operations strategy and management: *Operations Strategy*, by N Slack and M Lewis (2002, FT Prentice Hall).

f *Supply Chain Redesign: Transforming supply chains into integrated value systems* by R Handfield and E Nichols (2002, FT Prentice Hall).

g *Value Nets: Breaking the supply chain to unlock hidden profits* by D Bovet, J Martha and Adrian J Slywotsky (2000, Wiley).

h *Valuing Roles: How to establish relative worth* by Michael Armstrong and Ann Cummins (2008, Kogan Page) – includes job evaluation.

i Collaborative event management, supply chain sourcing: see **www.ciltuk,org.uk** and **www.cips.org**.

j Risk, general: *Against the Gods: The remarkable story of risk* by Peter Bernstein (1998, Wiley); financial: *The Handbook of Risk* edited by Ben Warwick (2003, IMCA).

k Public sector: traditionally, the best source material on how the public sector actually functions is the BBC's 'Yes, Minister' and 'Yes, Prime Minister' written by Antony Jay and Jonathan Lynn. To these must be added *Salmon Fishing in the Yemen* by Paul Torday (2007, Weidenfeld & Nicolson).

15B Further reading

Berry, C and Berry, R (2014) Better the Devil – a response to Gus O'Donnell's 'Better Government', *The Political Quarterly*, 85 (1)

Bouchal, P and McCrae, J (April 2013) *Financial Leadership for Government*, Institute for Government, London

The Cabinet Office (2013, 18 April) Capabilities Plan, The Cabinet Office, London

Coyle, D, *GDP: A brief but affectionate history* (2014), Princeton University Press

Dod's Parliamentary Companion and *Dod's Civil Service Companion*, London

Forrester, J (1961) *Industrial Dynamics*, Pegasus Communications, Waltham, MA

Fulford, B, Peile, R and Carroll, H (2012) *Essential Values-Based Practice: Clinical stories linking science with people*, Cambridge University Press, Cambridge

Goldacre, B (2014) I Think You'll Find It's a Bit More Complicated Than That, Fourth Estate, London

Goldsmith, Oliver (1770) *The Deserted Village*

Gray, J (2014) The Liberal delusion, *Prospect*, 23 September

John, P (2013) Experimentation, behaviour change and public policy, *The Political Quarterly*, 84 (2)

Judt, T (2010) *Ill Fares the Land*, Penguin Press, New York

The Jury Team (2009) *The End of the Party*, The Jury Team

The Jury Team (2010) *Working Together for the People Politicians Forgot*, The Jury Team (General Election Policy Document)

King, A and Crewe, I (2013) *The Blunders of our Governments*, Oneworld, London

Lambert, R (2013) Degrees of Debt – the student loans scheme is unsustainable, *Prospect*, May

Lincoln (2012) Directed by Steven Spielberg

Livingstone, D (1857) *Missionary Travels and Researches in South Africa*; (1865) *Narrative of an Expedition to the Zambezi and its Tributaries*; (1874) *The Last Journals of David Livingstone in Central Africa from 1865 to his Death*, Murray, London.

Marsh, I (2013) The decline of democratic governance, *The Political Quarterly*, 84 (2)

McGuffog, T (2011) Improving value and certainty in defence procurement, *Journal of Public Money & Management*, November

McGuffog, T et al. (2009) *Value Chain Management: Developing a more valuable and certain future*, CILT (in conjunction with CIPS & GS1), London

O'Donnell, G (2013) Better government, *The Political Quarterly*, **84** (3)
Owen, D (2008) *In Sickness and In Power*, Methuen, London
Radjou, N and Prabhu, J, *Frugal Innovation: How to do more with less* (2015), *The Economist*, London
'Reform' Think Tank (July 2013) Complete Modernisation of our Public Services, 'Reform' Think Tank, London
Sandell, M (2013) *What Money Can't Buy: The moral limits of markets*, Penguin, Harmondsworth
Searle, R (1989) *Slightly Foxed but Still Desirable: The wicked world of book collecting*, Souvenir Press, London
Seddon, J (2008) *Systems Thinking in the Public Sector*, Triarchy Press, Axminster
Seddon, J (2014) *The Whitehall Effect*, Triarchy Press, Axminster
Smith, A (1776) *An Inquiry into the Nature and Causes of the Wealth of Nations*, The Glasgow Edition (1976), Oxford University Press
Tett, G (2013) *The Silo Effect*, Simon & Schuster, New York
Toolis, K (2013) *The Confessions of Gordon Brown*, Play

INDEX

Page numbers in *italic* indicate figures or tables.

aircraft, building and maintaining   143–44
   see also identity
alternative dispute resolution (ADR)   169
articles/papers (on)
   'Better government' (*The Political Quarterly*, 2013)   111
     see also O'Donnell, G
   'The decline of democratic governance' (*The Political Quarterly*, 2013)   110
   'Degrees of Debt – the student loans scheme is unsustainable' (*Prospect*, 2013)   109
   '*The End of the Party*' (The Jury Team, 2009)   110–11
   'Improving value and certainty in defence procurement' (*Journal of Public Money & Management*, 2011)   82, 108 *see also* McGuffog, T
   'The Liberal delusion' (*Prospect Magazine*, 2014)   111 *see also* Gray, J
   Working Together for the People Politicians Forgot (The Jury Team, 2010)   111
arts value chains   130–34
   core purpose of   130
   differing   131–32
   issues for   132–34
   objectives of   130–31
automotive value chain (and)   49–55
   core purpose of   49
   factory supplier value chain   51–52
   generating/fulfilling orders with speed and certainty   53–55, *54*
   high-end luxury value chain   53, *54*
   issues   55
   measures for   51
   objectives of   50–51
   plans for   51
   retuning the current value chain   52
   strategy for   49–50

Barclay, W   17
barcodes   135, 141, 142, 145, 157
   see also identity
   and Global Trade Identification Number (GTIN)   136–37
Berners-Lee, T   140–41

The Blunders of our Governments   107
Bouchal, P   109
Burns, R   133
   and 'The Book-Worms'   133
business process analysis (BPA) tools   164

Centre for Effective Dispute Resolution   169
chapter notes/references (for)
   health and core value chains   77
   introduction   12
   and key references/further reading   218–24
   managing uncertainty   197
   overarching values   16–17
   value chain collaboration and competition   175
   value in value chain management   30
charities   *see* voluntary and charitable sector value chains
Chartered Institute of Logistics and Transport (CILT)   107
   website of value   9
collaboration   29, 50, 70, 81, 118, 126, 181, 190
   and competition   3, 9, 45, 58, 165–76, 178, 212
collaborative framework agreement (CFA)   168–69
Comte-Sponville, A   17
constructing sound value chain process and data architectures (and)   149–64
   defining a sound data architecture (through)   156–60, *158*, *159*, *160*
   identities   157
   master data   157–60, *158*, *159*, *160*
   messages   156
   financial flows   161–652
   plan to payment process   151, 153, *152*, *153*–54, *154*, 154–6
   recommendations   162
   single window   161
   structuring the process architecture and business processes involved   150–51
   value chain process analysis and driving business change   163–64 *see also subject entry*

cost-benefit
    analysis 26, 64
    relationships 192
Coyle, D 23
Crewe, I 107

defence equipment (material) value
        chain 77–84
    analysis and some solutions 79–84
    core purpose of 77
    measures/targets/KPIs/SLAs 79
    objectives 78
    plans 78
    strategy for 77
The Deserted Village 108–09
disabled persons 122–26, *123*
    and SportsAble Project 123–26
discounted cash flow (DCF) 27
dynamic management of projects and
        initiatives (DMPI) (and)
        198–208, 210
    application to financial investment
        and value chain operations
        management 207–08
    conclusion 208
    methodology and objectives for
        199–203, *203*, *204*, *205*, *206*
        contract cost 200
        performance 199–200
        through-life cost 200
        timelines 200
        trade-offs 200–201, *201*

The Economics of Innocent Fraud 34
effective and integrated value chain
        planning (and) 176–81
    chapter summary 177
    dynamic planning 177–79
    integrated business planning
        179–81, *181*
Electronic Business, UK Council
        for 84
electronic point of sale scanning
        (EPOS) 189–90
electronics value chain 55–59
    analysis 58–59
    core purpose of 56
    measures/targets/KPIs for 57
    objectives of 56–57
    plan for 57
    strategy for 56
Energy and Climate Change, Department
        for 98, 102
Environment Agency 98
European Union *see also* legislation (EU)

figures
    the 21st-century value chain *18*
    customer-supplier role model for joint
        value chain management *153*
    disabled person's value chain *123*
    distribution of risks *186*
    dynamic acquisition – balance
        example *206*
    dynamic acquisition – demand
        example *204*
    dynamic acquisition – supply
        example *205*
    dynamic project and uncertainty
        management matrix *203*
    financial value chain: simplistic map of
        complexity *36*
    Forrester effect *189*
    health value chain master data:
        sources of information *160*
    integrated business planning *181*
    managing trade-offs *201*
    new improved order search and
        booking system *54*
    objectives to plan to payment *152*
    role model for VC communications *154*
    simple e-business: the complex order
        159
    the simple order *158*
Financial Leadership for Government 109
Financial Times (and) 37, 143
    Good Value (Book of the Year, 2009)
        40
    report on governance 39–40
    report on technology experience of
        bank directors (2015) 35
    top four global brands (May 2015) 58
financial value chain (and) 31–41
    analysis 35–40, *36*
    conclusion 40
    core purpose of 31
    good value 40
    issues 33–35
    objectives 32
    performance measures 33
    plan 33
    proposals 40–41
    strategy 32
Food, Agriculture and Rural Affairs,
        Department for (DEFRA) 11, 98
food value chain (and) 41–49
    analysis 44–45
    core purpose of 41
    goals 46–47
    measures/targets/KPIs 43–44
    objectives 42–43

Index

plan   43
retail (and)   45–49
    goals   46–47
    retailer core purpose   46
    strategy   47
    strategy   42
forecasting organizations, analysis of relative success of (*Sunday Times*, 2014)   179–80
foreign exchange (FOREX)   37
Forrester, J   188
Forrester effect   171, *189*
Frugal Innovation: How to do more with less   25

Galbraith, J K   34
garbage in garbage out (GIGO)   180
Garland, R   119
Gent, Sir C   140
Global Standards 1 (GS1)   136
Global Trade Identification Number (GTIN)   137
Good Value (*Financial Times* Book of the Year, 2009)   40
Goldacre, B   108
Goldsmith, O   108
The Gospel According to Luke   17
Gray, J   111
Green, S   40
gross domestic product (GDP)   22, 23, 61, 106

health and care   2, 62, 100, 104, 213
Health and Care Excellence, National Institute for (NICE)   70
health and care value chains (and)   65–77
    see also National Health Service (NHS)
    core purpose of   65
    measures/targets/KPIs for   66–69
    objectives for   65–66
    plan for   66
    strategy for   65
    suggested improvement opportunities   72–75
Hospice Movement   107, 117
How Adam Smith Can Change your Life   17
human values   15–17

I Think You'll Find It's a Bit More Complicated than That   108
identity (and)   135–48
    banking   141–42
    barcodes and GTIN   135, 136–37
    a better future   145–46
    building and maintaining aircraft   143–44
    defence   145
    electronic business and its history   138–41
    electronic tags and RFID   142
    healthcare identification   142–43
    master data   137–38
    need to do better   146–48
    problems for the elderly   147–48
Ill Fares the Land   109
In Sickness and in Power   108
Industrial Dynamics   188
An Inquiry into the Nature and Causes of the Wealth of Nations   108
immigrants   2, 4, 15, 61, 103
introduction   8–12, *11–12*

Jenkins, J   119
John, P   110
Judt, T   109

Keynesian language   25
King, A   107

Lambert, R   109
legislation (EU)
    directives on water   92, 94
    Restriction of Hazardous Substances and Waste Electrical and Electronic Equipment (WEEE)   59
    Treaty on the Functioning of the European Union (Articles 101 and 102)   165–66
legislation (UK)
    Competition Act (1998)   165
    Enterprise Act (2002)   165
    Finance Act (1980)   139
    Rule of Law   103–04
    Water Act (2014)   94
The Little Book of Big Expenses: How to live the MP lifestyle   111
Livingstone, D   10, 12

McCrae, J   109
McGuffey, W H   15–16
McGuffey's Eclectic Reader   15
McGuffog, T   107–08
managing uncertainty   182–97
    attitudes to uncertainty, opportunity and risk   191–92, *192*
    definitions (of)   185–87, *186*
        interest   187
        opportunity   186–87
        profit   187
        risk   187
        uncertainty   185–86

Index

managing uncertainty *Continued*
   integrated planning and risk methodology 193–96
   introduction to 182–85
   risk lists and matrices 196–97
   uncertainty explored 188–90, *189*
   uncertainty and lack of understanding 191
Marsh, I 110
mission and vision 19
modern value chains *see* arts value chains; automotive value chain; defence equipment (material) value chain; electronics value chain; financial value chain; food value chain; health and care value chains; passenger transport – rail, road, air, sea; public sector value chain; reform of key institutions; sports club value chain; voluntary and charitable sector value chains *and* water value chain

National Audit Office 76, 103, 107, 114
National Health Service (NHS) 26, 67–76, 103
   Connecting for Health 191
   and healthcare identification 142–43
   proposals for 75–76
   suggested improvement opportunities for 72–75
      improvements 72–73
      strengths 74
      value chain management 73
      weaknesses 74–75
   value chain 69–72
      core principles 69
      objectives 72
      strategy 69–71
net added value (NAV) 22, 23–24
net present value NPV 27–28
net value (NV) 22
NIMBUS internet system 190

O'Donnell, G 111
On the Wealth of Nations 17
Open Systems Interconnection (OSI) 191
the optimal sequence of decisions *18*, 19–21
   and the decision sequence 19
   summary for 19
O'Rourke, P J 17
overarching values (and) 13–17
   democracy and citizenship 15
   ethical and fundamental 13–14
   relative values 14–16
   summary 13
   a valuable conclusion 16
   value chain partners 14
Owen, D 108

passenger transport – rail, road, air, sea 84–89
   core purpose of 84
   and issues 87–89
   measures/targets/KPIs for 87
   objectives for 85–86
   plan for 86–87
   strategy for 84–85
Picasso, P 132
Porter, E 10
Prabhu, J 25
practical exercises in value chain management 215–17
   1. select two value chains 215–16
   2. select an organization 216
   3. select a paper or online form 216
   4. pick an initiative or project 216–17
   5. select an organization in need of reform 217
Project Mala 119–22
   values 120–22
Public Money and Management (2011) 82
public sector value chain (and) 60–65
   analysis and proposals 63–65
      example for 64–65
   core purpose of 60
   issues 62–63
   measures/targets/KPIs for 61
   objectives 61
   plan 61
   priorities for value chain management in 65
   strategy for 60

Radjou, N 25
realizing value and value chain management (and) 1–7
   executive summary 1–2
   summary of chapters 2–4
   value 5–7
references 218–24 *see also* chapter notes/references
reform of key institutions (and of) 99–115
   government value chain 99–111
      core purpose 99–100
      democratic values and objectives 101–07
      strategy 100–101
   our democratic value chain 111–15

Index

RFID tags (and)   83, 160
  electronic tags   142
  ID systems   157
risk   191–96, *192*
  addiction   192
  attitude   192
  averse   192
  aware   192
  methodology (and integrated planning)   193–96
Roberts, R   17
Royal National Lifeboat Institution (RNLI)   107, 116

Sandell, M   108
scandals and scares/traumas   48
  horse meat scandal   48
  Lehman Brothers   39
Schweitzer, A   16
Searle, R   133
Seddon, J   110
A Short Treatise on the Great Virtues   17
The Silo Effect   189
Slightly Foxed but Still Desirable: The wicked world of book collecting   133
Smith, A   9–10, 12, 14, 16, 17, 108, 190
sports club value chain (and)   127–30
  core purpose of   128
  means   129
  objectives   128
  opportunities   129
  risks   130
  values   128
SportsAble Project   123–26
  analysis   125–26
  value chain   125
  values   126
standard(s)   6, 15, 45, 51, 141, 143–44, 162
  bodies and inspectors   55
  for the Exchange of Product Model Data (ISO STEP)   143
  Global Standards 1 (GS1)   136, 137, 157
  of governance   118
  STEP   157
  SWIFT   157
  TRADACOMS   140
  for water   92, 94
success, twelve practical steps to   209–10
SWAT – strengths, weaknesses, opportunities and threats   48
Systems Thinking in the Public Sector   110

tables
  attitudes to uncertainty, opportunity and risk   *192*
  value analysis   *11–12*
Tett, G   189
TRADACOMS   136, 139–40
TRADANET   140
  tender and development   136
Transport, Department for   86, 88, 98, 213–14

United Kingdom (UK)
  Council for Electronic Business (UKCeb)   136
  Home Office and best practice   196
  Parliament   60, 106, 113–14
    Members of   100, 102, 103
  Trading Data Communications Standard (1982)   139–40
  Treasury Orange Book   187
United Nations (UN)
  and Simpl.e.business principles   139
  standard for ebusiness communications   136
United States (US)   15–16, 140
  see also immigrants
  and American values   15
  FBI and financial fraud   37
  outstanding equity values in (2008)   39

Valery, P   115
valuable steps   *see* success, twelve practical steps to *and* value chain research and development
value   9, 24
value chain collaboration and competition issues   165–75
  effective collaboration and competition (and)   170–75
    categories of value chain relationship   172–74
    process for effective collbration   174–75
  legal issues   165–68 *see also* legislation (EU) *and* legislation (UK)
  practical issues: collaboration, communication and costs   168–70
value chain management (VCM)   *see* practical exercises in value chain management; realizing value and value chain management *and* the value in value chain management
Value Chain Management   37

Index

Value Chain Management: Developing a more valuable and certain future 107
value chain management mapping and references 218–21
value chain maps/mapping 210, 218–19
value chain process analysis and driving business change 163–64
  and emergence of business process analysis and mapping tools 164
  end goal: the thought-through value chain 164
  traditional approach to 163–64
value chain research and development, proposed areas for 211–14
value chains *see* arts value chains; constructing sound value chain process and data architectures; sports club value chain *and* voluntary and charitable sector value chains
the value in value chain management (and) 22–29
  conclusions 29
  definitions 22
  earned value management (EVM) 28
  frugal innovation 25
  net present value (NPV) 27–28
  stocks and flows 27
  summary 22
  transfer prices 29
  value chain linkages and interactions 25
  value chain management measures 25–26
  valuing human life 26

voluntary and charitable sector value chains (and) 116–27
  see also SportsAble Project
  analysis 118–19
  core purpose 117
  measures of performance 118
  objectives 117
  overview of 126–27
  plans 117
  Project Mala 119–22
  strategy 117
  values/wider community values 122–23, *123*

Water Services Regulation Authority (Ofwat) 11, 15, 90, 93, 94
water value chain: structure and added value 89–98
  analysis of/proposals for 92
    aspects of supply 92–93
    challenges to value chain decisions 97–98
    customer perspective 96–97
    investors 94
    markets 95–96
    regulation and incentives 93–94
    water and the environment 98
  core purpose of 89–90
  measures for 92
  objectives for 91–92
  strategy and practice for 90–91
The Wealth of Nations 9, 12, 17, 190
What Money Can't Buy: The moral limits of markets 108
The Whitehall Effect 110
World Trade Organization (WTO) talks 49
World Wide Web 140–41